Drowning In Memories

Drowning In Memories

Norm Sawyer

Norm Sawyer

© 2022 Norm Sawyer
ISBN 10: 1-988226-44-9
ISBN 13: 978-1-988226-49-1

Cover Art: Kane Sawyer
Cover Graphics: Lee MacLennan
Black And White Photography: Norm Sawyer

Published by

First Page Solutions
Kelowna, BC, Canada

DEDICATION

Adam and Troy, who are good citizens of this
earth.

CONTENTS

FOREWORD

I have often been struck by how Norm turns the Word of God over and over, carefully considering it from different angles, asking questions, seeking answers, but never holding on so tight to his learning that he stops being curious. Having a cup of coffee (or many cups!) with him has always included a rousing discussion about his latest adventure into scripture. I am excited that Norm has continued these conversations through his writing.

In his latest book, *Drowning in Memories,* Norm explores the complexities of our past, our future, and the important work of forgiveness while reframing our memories through the lens of scripture.

Forgiveness is such a complicated concept. Our humanity demands justice for the wrongs that have been leveled against us; we cry for restitution and often wish to go back to the time before our sorrow. But this is not life. Life continues forward, away from those traumas, despite our grief. How do we live the abundant life God has promised us when we are shackled to the past?

Drowning in Memories seeks to answer this question. Norm invites us to lay down the burden of our past and walk into the freedom God has promised.

So, dear reader, pour yourself a cup of coffee, pull up a chair, and join the conversation.

-Bernadette Sciortino

PART ONE:

DROWNING IN MEMORIES

Drowning In Memories

We can get caught up in the memories of the past, and think that we should have done things differently, then allow that thought to discredit our lives to this point. God says "Today is the day of salvation." Thank God for today and stop drowning in memories you cannot change.

DROWNING IN MEMORIES

Proverbs 10:7 We have happy memories of the godly, but the name of a wicked person rots away.

Ecclesiastes 7:10 **Do not say, "Why were the old days better than these?" For it is not wise to ask such questions.** I once wrote, and I still believe, "The only good thing about the good old days is that they are gone," especially when the old days are the only thing a person thinks about. People can become so trapped in the past that they no longer try to live today.

It is much easier to deal with memories that are pleasant and joyful because they sometimes encourage us to believe in an optimistic future. Good memories are helpful as they can inspire us to realize that things can get better. It is a harder journey for a lot of people to deal with and try to manage the hurts that horrific memories bring back in living colour. The relenting torment of these aching recollections keep people from advancing beyond their ever-present thoughts of how they were poorly treated. Continually thinking about the old hurts, and rehashing the events that created the dysfunction in their present lives, will have an unnatural control of their mind and will give no room for peace to be found.

The difficulty of being reconciled with our painful history can be overwhelming for some people and a never-ending torment for others. We are now seeing how the memories of the First Nation's children who were forced to attend residential schools are still feeling the repercussions they suffered. Those children are now elderly people who are still hurting. The effects on these people and their culture have got to be reconciled or the pain will continue to be a generational curse. The brutality and shaming practices that were allowed to be used upon these children at the time, were inhumane, and cruel. Yet, these people were expected to live inspired lives and function normally once returned to their homes. How could they not become maladaptive in their plight to function when they had so many questions that needed answers as to why they had been treated like a burden society had to rid themselves of.

The anguish that is suffered within the souls

and spirits of anyone who has memories of being brutalized makes it hard for them to even believe there is healing for better things. Healing in the spirit is also needed as much as healing within the soul. Ex.6:9 **So Moses spoke thus to the children of Israel; but they did not heed Moses, because of anguish of spirit and cruel bondage.** Depressive and painful memories will keep many wallowing in hurtful reminiscence while keeping them stagnant from moving ahead. We have no choice but to reconcile with our hurtful past because if we do not face that pain with God's healing power, that dark shadow will negatively control our thoughts causing a repeat performance within the next generation.

Breaking this bondage will take the light of God that can stab any darkness and rip apart the gloom that has enveloped a heart and mind. However, we have to want that healing with all of our hearts. God's righteous fire burns everything and that includes the injustices we have suffered throughout our lives. I, for one, have had to forgive the events of my childhood to be able to live a healthy and meaningful life today. I had to forgive the brutality and abuse that my father dispensed on my mother, siblings, and myself. I have written extensively on the subject of my father's inability to have loved, nurtured, and protected his family. We cannot go back and fix the problem at the point where the torture took place, but with the Lord's forgiving grace we can be healed from the point where we choose to forgive. Matt. 6:14 **For if you forgive other people when they sin against you, your heavenly Father will also forgive you.**

The problem for many who continue choosing the companion of old shadows that darken the present noonday brightness is that they will rewrite scenarios in their minds and will end up with a patchwork of selective memories that are distorting the real events that took place. The children of Israel had been set free by God but in their hearts, they were still slaves to their past. Num. 11:5 **We remember the fish we used to eat for free in Egypt. And we had all the cucumbers, melons, leeks, onions, and garlic we wanted. 6 But now we have lost our appetite; we never see anything but this manna!** The manna was the healing bread that the Lord had provided each day for the collective healing of a nation. Yes, it was a daily food provision, but the morning reminder as the manna was gathered demonstrated that God their provider could meet anything needed to live in wholeness. However, as is today, if we do not accept God's healing and step into His redemptive health plan with an honest heart the result will be as it was with the children of Israel - an insipid idea of existence.

The choice is ours. We can either swim and bathe in the anointed love of God's present affection that will eventually heal all pain and hurts. Or, we can drown in the infectious waters of hurtful memories that move like the creatures in nightmares coming from beneath ready to bring us into a hell of loneliness. The Lord's salvation is too precious a gift to be ignored as the way back from our painful past. If we hand over one hurt after another until the healing balm of Christ's sacrifice makes us whole, we will eventually be healed. There are enough people in this world living with a shadow-sickness that gets darker as the days go by. We who are in Christ can live in the light of God's healing. Ex. 15:26b **For I am the LORD who heals you**. We just have to want it. In Jesus name, Lord God, help us call on Your name for the grace needed to choose life. Amen!

THE DARK SIDE

Proverbs 4:18 But the path of the righteous is like the bright morning light, growing brighter and brighter until full day.

Historians have recorded volumes depicting paintings, books, movies, plays, essays and every other form of recording man's journey, that describe the dark side of the human condition. Why is that? Because we know darkness intimately. Adam and Eve did not do us any favours by allowing us to know and become intimately fettered to darkness and the resulting death through sin. Overcoming dark thoughts requires a massive amount of work because we know how bad sin can get, and how awful it is. History has proven that we cannot fix the dreadful shortcomings that reside within us. Jer. 17:9 **The human heart is the most deceitful of all things, and desperately wicked. Who really knows how bad it is?** Being focused on darkness and evil will keep us living feverishly with unimaginative minds, resulting in repetitive acting out of sinfulness, and living within iniquity's control.

I was reading an article that said it takes five to seven positive thoughts to overcome one negative thought that has taken root in our soul or psyche. That amount of positiveness is a lot of mental work that has to be done to have a positive outcome on a particular event in one's life. No wonder the Word of the Lord admonishes us to think about the good things worthy of thought. Phil. 4:8 **And now, dear brothers and sisters, one final thing. Fix your thoughts on what is true, and honorable, and right, and pure, and lovely, and admirable. Think about things that are excellent and worthy of praise.** Staying focused on God's integral goodness will give us life and help us stay out of gloomy places.

In the book of Ruth, we read how after Naomi's husband and two sons died, Naomi gave credence to the idea that this tragedy was a judgment from God upon herself. Her wounded spirit interpreted those calamitous events as a form of punishment. Ruth 1:13b **For it grieves me much for your sakes that the hand of the LORD is gone out against me.** When darkness sets in, the battle for the mind is a battle in earnest. Even after the length of time it took to travel back to her country with Ruth, Naomi had not shaken the dark spirit of self-blame. Ruth 1:20 **And she said unto them, Call me not Naomi, call me Mara: for the Almighty hath dealt very bitterly with me.** Naomi could only see her misery and needed a holy wind of righteous thoughts to help her navigate the grief that had become a weight of hurt that hung around her soul.

While this tragic family event was taking place in Naomi's life, a miracle of grace was happening at the same time. Naomi could not see it, but Ruth, a Moabite woman had risen in faith by declaring that Jehovah would be her God until death. Ruth 1:16b **Your people will be my people and your God my God. 17 Where you die I will die, and there will I be buried. May the LORD do so to me and more also if anything but death parts me from you.** Ruth had not only made a covenant with her mother-in-law to take care of her but also declared God to be her LORD.

Ruth's use of the name, LORD, (Jehovah) demonstrated that God was real to Ruth at this difficult time. Grief and loss made it hard for

Naomi to see the blessings right in front of her. I believe that Ruth had gleaned Godly insights into the power of the name Jehovah while married and living with her inlaws. Out of the darkness of life's harsh events, Ruth followed the only light she knew at the time, and He was the covenant God of Israel. Naomi needed a reawakening of the illumination that Ruth had believed for herself. Prov. 4:18 **But the path of the righteous is like the bright morning light, growing brighter and brighter until full day.**

We are in desperate need of a kinsman redeemer to deliver us from our prison of unsanctified existence, which can easily bring us into a dark place. Thank God for the saving blood of Jesus, which sets us free from eternal death and our ever-increasing dysfunctions. If it does take five to seven positive thoughts to overcome negative influences in our life, then let us focus on the pure positive love of God that He has for every one of us. Let us dive into the Word of God, so we can be washed in the Shekinah glory of our Lord God. We can dispel the darkness that prowls at our doorsteps because we have the Lord within our hearts, making us through Christ, the

light of the world. Let us walk in that light. Matt.
5:14a **You are the light of the world.** Amen!

A LONELY PLACE

Proverbs 18:24 One who has unreliable friends soon comes to ruin, but there is a friend who sticks closer than a brother.

I prayed out loud, "Lord, what is wrong with me? What is this agitation boiling up in my soul?" I feel like I'm fighting something I cannot touch. I can almost catch glimpses of it in my spiritual peripheral vision, but it remains a mercurial shadow on the edges of thought. I'm convinced I see a pending storm with a gun barrel grey ceiling pressing down upon me, even while the sun is shining on every side. My eyes are focused on a bright and clear day, but my soul feels a darkened membrane stretching against my mind. Father, I just want to give up. "Am I depressed?" I asked. I questioned again, "Lord, can you tell me, what is agitating my soul?" I heard a soft, "You are lonely."

I said, "Everyone is lonely, we have been in restrictions and lockdowns for over two years. Besides, I have friends and lots to keep me busy."

Again, I heard, "You are lonely." How have I come to this lonely place? Is this one of the aspects of being human, where we must process and encounter the test we are shadowboxing? Do we have to go through a dire valley to understand the lessons being taught in our souls? This wretchedness is too real to ignore or escape its festering. Psalm 55:6 **I said, "Oh, that I had the wings of a dove! I would fly away and be at rest.** Where is our God who gives us rest?

Do I put on a mask and fake it till I make it? If I wear a mask, it will reveal what is within me by the mask I am using. If my mask is happiness, I am covering up the sadness within my heart. If my mask is bravery, I am hiding the cowardice at work in my conscience. If I wear the mask of confidence, I am hiding the fact that I feel like a cardboard cutout empty of substance. Psalm 69:3 **I am worn out calling for help; my throat is parched. My eyes fail, looking for my God.** Heavenly Father, I need a saviour, not a formula. I don't need three steps to overcome blah blah blah. I need to be heard in my moment of uncertainty. Are you there Lord?

Maybe this is a battle against demonic giants

whose shadows tower over my existence. Satan is the one who murders the visions of holy men who end up in lonely places. From this empty place, I received an illumination of thought. The Holy Spirit is listening to my groans. From out of the depths of my groanings is my sincere heart wanting God's affirmation of purpose and declaration of love. Rom. 8:26 **And the Holy Spirit helps us in our weakness. For example, we don't know what God wants us to pray for. But the Holy Spirit prays for us with groanings that cannot be expressed in words.** Even in a dark place, we look for light to find our way, while we call upon our Lord to send His healing oil that anoints our soul and resurrects our lives into the joy of relationship with our God.

Yes, Lord, I see there is life after being buried under the lies of the enemy. If we trust in your goodness and trust your leading, we can come out of dark places. For you are a friend to the downcast and a Lord to the needy. Prov. 18:24b **But there is a friend who sticks closer than a brother.** I will look to the heavens and hope again. For this dry place is but for a season. Our hope is in God, and He will sustain us with the love of His graciousness. The salvation of God is for all man, even the corrupt and inventors of evil. One drop of the Lord's blood can change the vilest of souls. Yes, Lord, there is hope in your grace.

As I prayed, God sent His healing oil through an anointed friend who ministered the majesty of the Holy Spirit upon my soul. Fragrant oil dripped upon my heart and I left the lonely place for the garden of God's Eden. I found other souls resting there. "Your battle is won," they shouted, "You have been tried and found to be alive in the grace of God's divine love." Thank you, Lord, for your goodness of heart and for delivering me from the lonesome place of endless wastelands. I will remember to put on the whole armour of God, that I may extinguish the spears of burning darkness. Lord, you are good and worthy to be praised. Thank you, God, I am home. Amen!

REVERSING THE CURSE

Proverbs 26:2 As the bird by wandering, as the swallow by flying, so the curse causeless shall not come.

The subject of reversing a curse in one's life is too spooky, odd, or even out-there for some Christians to believe possible, and that is sad since the Lord has given us the ability and blessing to do so. Matt. 18:18 **Truly I tell you, whatever you bind on earth will have been bound in heaven, and whatever you loose on earth will have been loosed in heaven.** We can bind the curses that follow our family, but it will take faith and God's instruction to get it done. We have to use our faith in Christ to become free of whatever binds us. James 2:26 **For as the body without the spirit is dead, so faith without works is dead also.**

The reason for not dealing with some unexplained hurts, bondages, memories, and repeated failures in our lives is just not wanting to face these devils that have come to accuse our hearts. Some of us have become weary and wary of the whole thing. I would encourage you to try one more time and trust the Lord's word by using this powerful gift of deliverance.

My first encounter with the need to deal with a hurtful event from my past would come around every September to October. I would go through the most horrible feelings of depression, worthlessness, self-hatred, and sluggishness to the point of craving death for relief. If I would have been able to explode from the inside out and all my particles were to spread throughout the universe, I would still not have found the release from the anguish and self-hatred I carried.

Once November came around, I was fine. What curse was I living under and how could I get rid of it? Even after I was saved in Christ, I would still experience this yearly unwanted visitation in my life. The difference was that now I had a way to be healed because I believed in the healing power of the Lord Jesus.

I was praying and asking God to reveal to me the root of this yearly battle when I felt I should call my mother and ask her if I had been conceived out of wedlock. Thank you, Lord, for my courageous and loving mother who confessed to me during that phone call that, yes, I was a year old when my parents were finally married.

I had found the accusation the enemy of my soul was using to keep me in self-hatred. Satan was using the broken law of fornication to try and kill me from the first day of my conception. Duet. 23:2 **A bastard shall not enter into the congregation of the LORD; even to his tenth generation shall he not enter into the congregation of the LORD.**

Thank God that there are no illegitimate children on this earth; there are only sinful parents. Praise the Lord that the sins of these parents have been paid for in full by the blood of our Saviour Jesus Christ.

Is the devil determined to destroy your life? We better know that Satan is cursing us and our existence all the time. Psalm 10:7 **His mouth is full of cursing and deceit and fraud: under his tongue is mischief and vanity.** Psalm 109:17 **He loved to pronounce a curse may it come back on him. He found no pleasure in blessing may it be far from him. 18 He wore cursing as his garment; it entered into** his body like water, into his bones like oil. 19 May it be like a cloak wrapped about him, like a belt tied forever around him. 20 May this be the LORD's payment to my accusers, to those who speak evil of me.

The weapon that I have learned to use is the act and participation of communion. Who am I showing the Lord's death to? Who am I reminding that I have been saved and completely delivered? I am showing it to the enemy who cannot stand in the presence of Christ's holy blood. 1Cor. 11:23 **For I have received of the Lord that which also I delivered unto you, That the Lord Jesus the same night in which he was betrayed took bread: 24 and when he had given thanks, he brake it, and said, "Take, eat: this is my body, which is broken for you: this do in remembrance of me." 25 After the same manner also he took the cup, when he had supped, saying, "This cup is the new testament in my blood: this do ye, as oft as ye drink it, in remembrance of me." 26 For as often as ye eat this bread, and drink this cup, ye do show the Lord's death till he come.**

The key here is the deliverance that comes

from Christ's words, 'Do this in remembrance of me.' The doing of communion is the act of faith on your part because of who you are in Christ, and the result is the testament of His blood covered once and for all the events of your hurtful past.

The communion becomes a reference point as to when you actually dealt with the traumas of your life. When a new accusation arises, your faith will say, "No, this is covered by the blood forever and I walk in that freedom."

I have had great personal deliverance from using this powerful and spiritual gift that God has given us to use as a weapon against the devil and other sicknesses. Today, I love the months of September and October. I am free from all the terrible feelings I used to experience and have learned to deal with any memory that comes to haunt my soul by partaking through faith, in the act of worship and communion. Isa. 12:4 **And in that day shall ye say, Praise the LORD, call upon his name, declare his doings among the people, make mention that his name is exalted.** Amen.

I REMEMBER WHEN

Proverbs 16:3 Commit to the LORD whatever you do, and he will establish your plans.

In 1969, I remember when a gallon of gasoline rose in price from forty-five cents to fifty cents per gallon. A lot of people were fearful that they were not going to make it financially. An eleven percent increase in cost at that time was unheard of. The feeling that the sky was falling - because so many people were saying that very thing, made the times seem uncertain concerning the future and everyone's well-being. Of course, looking back, the sky did not fall, and a lot of worrying and unnecessary suffering of the mind that took place - was for naught. Matt. 6:25 **Therefore I tell you, do not worry about your life, what you will eat or drink; or about your body, what you will wear. Is not life more than food, and the body more than clothes?**

The above scripture admonishes us not to worry or stress when times get hard or are perceived to be overwhelming. This is still a good lesson to take to heart. Lately, many people are expressing their fears concerning the future, and they are making general statements like, "I remember when things used to be much better than today. "Maybe it is the age group that I am in, but I hear that statement voiced a lot. The words "I remember when" seem to come out as an expression of surrendering to life's difficult changes which give rise to a person's feeling of helplessness to do anything about their circumstances. So, they just sigh and say, "I remember when life seemed to be much easier to handle." Eccl. 7:10 **Do not say, "Why were the old days better than these?" For it is not wise to ask such questions.** I'm not sure if life was ever easier or if we are choosing a false memory that we find comfort in because we have survived life to this point. But now, because we do not know the future or the challenges that are coming, we are faced with a fresh new set of anxieties. Therefore, we stew in the thoughts of "I remember when."

What I do know is that wringing our hands and fretting about all the problems coming upon the earth is not good for our inner peace or our ability to be positive toward our future. Thinking constantly and fearing what we cannot control will affect a person's emotional well-being and the health of their body. The stress will eventually cause sickness and disease throughout their whole body. Job 21:6 **When I remember, I am dismayed, and shuddering seizes my flesh.** This is not a healthy way to live or plan life's goals. Therefore, we have to commit our ways to the Lord so that we get real answers for planning our life in the peace and health God has for us. Prov. 16:3 **Commit to the LORD whatever you do, and he will establish your plans.**

God's salvation is for our whole lives, which includes our spirit, soul, and body. The Lord is always ready to provide what we need when we ask of Him. But, there seems to be an indication from God's word that worry and pining for the past interferes with the flow of the blessings coming our way. Worry and stress will weaken our faith in believing that God is for us. Faith is courageous and it humbly steps forward to receive from God what we need to live victoriously. Stress and worry are born in fear, and God has not given us the spirit of fear. Authentic faith believes the love that God has for us, and in the light of God's love, there is no darkness or fear. 1John 4:18a **There is no fear in love, but perfect love casts out fear.**

Our Heavenly Father is not against us remembering events from the old days that bring fond recollections and expressions of gratefulness toward God. The Lord wants us to remember who He is. He is the mighty creator who is here for us and He wants us to remember the wonderful miracles He has given us throughout our life. Habitually remembering the Lord throughout our time on earth will help us remember Him when the days are hard. Eccl. 12:1 **Remember also your Creator in the days of your youth, before the evil days come and the years draw near of which you will say, "I have no pleasure in them."** Isn't that what people are saying when they say, "I remember when life was better than it is now." They are saying, "I have no pleasure in the days God has given me." No, Saints. We need to be grateful for the life God gave us and to use our lives to bring gracious pleasantness to a hopeless world full of woes. Lam. 3:21 **This I recall to my mind, therefore have I hope. 22 It is of the LORD'S mercies that we are not**

consumed, because his compassions fail not.

We can sit back and bemoan the fact that things are not as they were. But I would rather remember that when my life was a mess, God pulled me out of that ugly nightmare to live for Him today. I remember when I was an alcoholic and God delivered me from that addiction so that I could face the challenges of today in His strength. I could sit around remembering a lot of things that are probably worth forgetting, but I would rather remember the blessings and opportunities I have had throughout my life since Jesus became my Lord and Saviour. I remember when I was lost, but now I am found in Christ. That is something to remember. Amen!

FAMINE IN PARADISE

Proverbs 11:3 The integrity of the upright will guide them, but the crookedness of the treacherous will destroy them.

Genesis 47:4 **And they said to Pharaoh, "We have come to stay in the land for a while because there is no grazing land for your servants' sheep, since the famine in the land of Canaan has been severe. So now, please let your servants settle in the land of Goshen."**

How can there be a famine in the land of promise? I thought God would make sure nothing bad or difficult would happen to me once I signed on the dotted salvation line? We are being unrealistic if we think we will coast through this life with no battles to overcome in our walk with God. We have an enemy whose main intention toward all man is destruction, mayhem, and death.

Sometimes Christians are befuddled when things go wrong in their lives - as if being in Christ solves all problems instantly. "Why am I having these troubles if God is on my side?" is a question often asked. In a lot of situations, we are having problems because God is with us. John 16:33 **These things I have spoken unto you, that in me ye might have peace. In the world ye shall have tribulation: but be of good cheer; I have overcome the world.**

Remember that a relationship with God is not an insurance policy for a perfect life, but rather, it is a blessed assurance of the fact that God is for us and in the end, we will come out victorious. However, going through life will have multiple challenges of all kinds. Some will be easy enough to overcome and some will become brutal battles with casualties.

As Christians, we will need our faith to defeat sickness, disease, and stress as many people in the world do. We will set goals throughout our life and will have ups and downs when the enemy of our soul throws a wicked curveball our way. We are in a world where many terrible events happen. But, we are not of the world where we face these events alone. We have the Lord in our hearts and on our side directing us through the valley of life's shadows. However, we do not stop and become residents in the valley of turmoil. Our life is hidden in Christ and we will resurrect to victory.

Rebekah was dealing with the fact that she could not conceive a child. If Rebekah was in covenant with God as her husband Isaac was, then why all the infertility problems? Didn't God promise Abraham that the whole world would be blessed because of Abraham's descendants? Gen. 22:18 **And through your descendants all the nations of the earth will be blessed—all because you have obeyed me.**

Relationship with the Lord is not a guarantee for easy living, but rather, a call to prayer and devotion with our God. The Lord will guide us toward conquering the giants before us when we ask for His help by faith. Gen. 25:21 **Isaac prayed to the Lord on behalf of his wife because she was childless. The Lord was receptive to his prayer, and his wife Rebekah conceived.**

King David was a man after God's heart, and yet, he had major battles after he inherited the promises of God concerning his reign. The Apostles had to overcome some of the most treacherous attacks on their character and physical bodies after they had been proclaimed the leaders of our faith. Historically, the cruelty perpetrated on the men and women of God has been outrageous and shameful, and yet, these saints belonged to God and battled forward. Heb. 10:32 **Remember the earlier days when, after you had been enlightened, you endured a hard struggle with sufferings.** All these people endured after the promises of Christ had been fulfilled in their lives.

Can there be a famine in the land of promise? Yes, but this should not stop us from proclaiming the promises of God. We should not stop drawing closer to the heart of our heavenly Father. When we keep our integrity during hard times, God will guide us through the mess. Prov. 11:3 **The integrity of the upright will guide them, but the crookedness of the treacherous will destroy them.** If there can be a famine in the land of promise while we walk in the blessings of the Lord, then imagine the devastating war-torn deprivation that is prevalent in the world system, where there is no hope, future, or restoration of the soul.

We who are in the Lord, always have a redemptive hope in our hearts. Christ, our beacon leads us through the battlefields of life where we are more than conquerors. We never need to worry, because the Lord will keep us and guide us to the very end. Psalm 48:14 **For that is what God is like. He is our God forever and ever, and he will guide us until we die.**

Norm Sawyer

WORKING THROUGH IT

Proverbs 4:23 Keep thy heart with all diligence; for out of it are the issues of life.

Over eight years ago, I covenanted with God, with His grace, that I would do my best to take care of my heart that misses a beat. Because of poor life choices, work-related stress, plus, bad eating habits, I caused my heart to become diseased and eventually I suffered a stroke. I have changed my lifestyle entirely, while I keep believing God to heal my heart, and restore it to its full natural capacity.

Whole and real foods have become my diet of choice, and I have been working out regularly at the gym and some of the exercise parks available in my area. Working through so many lifestyle changes has become a focus in my life. One of the keys that resulted in my present good health was knowing that I was always working through a phase of hardship to the eventual accomplishment I was after. Plus, I did not resent the slow progress that sometimes showed up. Zec.

36

4:10a **Do not despise these small beginnings, for the LORD rejoices to see the work begin.** It took a lot of effort and time, but it was truly worth it.

While working out at the gym, one of the noticeable regularities is that each person is working through something in their workout routine. Some are working through a new pain that occurred since they started exercising the muscles in a different part of their body. While many are working toward their goals of strength and weights that they set for themselves. Others are just working out how they are going to get through the first week of training while wheezing, grunting, moaning, and screaming, "I'm never coming back," or "I will get through this come hell or high water."

The overall theme is - everyone is working through something, and it is going to take more than just talk to get their weight-training and lifestyle changes done. It's going to take the diligence of heart and character to work through some of the difficulties that will be encountered. Prov. 4:23 **Keep thy heart with all diligence; for out of it are the issues of life.**

Every level of training brings new challenges, and it is no different in our walk with God. There will never be a time when we are not going through some kind of spiritual growth and strengthening in our faith. Phil. 3:13 **Brothers and sisters, I do not consider myself yet to have taken hold of it. But one thing I do: Forgetting what is behind and straining toward what is ahead, 14 I press on toward the goal for the prize of the upward call of God in Christ Jesus.**

Remember that the rain falls on the just and the unjust equally. There will be some hardships in life and that is part of living. However, we have our heavenly Father who will guide us through the difficulties. The Lord will help us stand by faith in the promises of His word.

The Apostle Paul who suffered extensively throughout his ministry had many reasons to give up but wrote that God had continually rescued him. 2Tim. 3:10 **You, however, know all about my teaching, my way of life, my purpose, faith, patience, love, endurance, 11 persecutions, sufferings—what kinds of things happened to me in Antioch, Iconium and Lystra, the persecutions I endured. Yet the Lord rescued**

me from all of them. Name it, and Paul went through it.

I don't know what you are going through right now, but please realize that you are travelling in a temporary place. You do not have to stop and live there for the rest of your life. You are walking through the valley of shadows because you are battling what life throws at you.

We are all working through something, and those who know their God will come out victorious. We will eventually see that we were growing from glory to glory. It may take time, but as in health training, it is worth it, because this holy training is of eternal value. God bless you and give you the strength to accomplish what the Lord has put in your heart to do.

Norm Sawyer

TURN YOUR FAITH BACK ON

Proverbs 2:8 He guards the paths of justice, and preserves the way of His saints.

Pope Francis wrote in his book, *Happiness in this life,* "A saint that is sad, is a sad excuse for a saint." He also wrote, "A gloomy disciple, is a disciple of gloom."

As believing saints and disciples in Christ, we should be the happiest people on earth. By the grace of God, we who are the saints of our Lord can bring hope to those who have lost their way in this ever-changing world. After all, we do have the Godhead living within our being, and the ability to be a heavenly-encouragement. These Godly blessings should be flowing out of our lives. Philemon 1:7 **For I have great joy and encouragement from your love, because the hearts of the saints have been refreshed through you, brother.**

Sometimes, we, the saints of the Lord, can become battle-weary and begin to lose the vision that was once clear and attainable in our hearts.

Tiredness in our soul can affect our faith and walk with God. Therefore, we have to choose to turn our faith back on. Gal. 6:9 **And let us not be weary in well doing: for in due season we shall reap, if we faint not.**

It is not up to your pastor, spouse, friend, or leader to get your faith working again - it is up to you and God. Where the aforementioned people can be helpful, is after you have chosen to turn your faith back on. Once you have prayed and asked God for help and strength, God can use these people to spark your soul into a faith-filled life.

God instructed Samuel the prophet to anoint David as the future king of Israel. David had conquered and killed the giant Goliath. He was on the heavenly fast-track for kingdom promotion. He was married to King Saul's daughter and living the good life in the palace. What could go wrong? Everything went wrong. David was falsely accused of treason and conspiracy to take the kingdom from Saul. He ended up hunted and running for his life. Now, having to live in caves and on the outskirts of villages in the hillsides, he had become a fugitive.

David must have prayed to God, and said, "I thought Samuel said I would be the king of Israel. I must have misunderstood. What did I do to deserve all this calamity in my life?" David had to encourage himself in the Lord and decide to turn his faith back on. He travelled to the town of Nob, and there, he was given Goliath's sword. 1Sam. 21:9 **"The priest replied, "The sword of Goliath the Philistine, whom you killed in the Valley of Elah, is here, wrapped in a cloth behind the ephod. If you want to take it for yourself, then take it, for there isn't another one here." "There's none like it!" David said. "Give it to me."**

God knows exactly what we need and when we need it. Just as David's faith needed encouragement, God reminded him of who he was, and that his future was still in God's hands. The sword David used to cut off Goliath's head was a timely reminder of all the victories that David had gone through.

David also remembered that the prophecies that had been spoken over him were still true and an inspiration to turn his faith back on. He was walking through the wilderness of his life, but

God met him and reminded him of the vision and promise for his life. Now, David could say with courage, Psalm 63:9 **But those who intend to destroy my life will go into the depths of the earth.** 10 **They will be given over to the power of the sword; they will become a meal for jackals.**

If gloominess and sadness have replaced your saintly shout in the Lord, then turn your faith back on. God knows what you need and that your strength will come through the joy of the Lord and faith in His name. Neh. 8:10b **For the joy of the LORD is your strength.**

What have you let go of that was once the vision of God for your life? How have you let the circumstances of life take your call, strength, and ministry away from the forefront of your mind and spirit? Turn your faith back on and get with God's eternal vision for your life.

We can count on God to preserve the dreams He sowed in our hearts when He created us. As saints in the Lord, we stay on the path God has laid out for us so that our life's purpose may be fulfilled. Prov. 2:8 **He guards the paths of justice, and preserves the way of His saints.**

There will be times when we fail, but our faith in the Lord can lift us above the failure and put the shout of victory back in our hearts.

As saints in Christ, we can help many overcome the sadness that is prevalent in this world. May our God remind us of the giants we have slain and the victories we have won in the Lord's name. Yes, we are more than conquerors, through Christ, who gives us the victory. Amen!

LABAN'S LABOR LAWS

Proverbs 10:16 The wage of the righteous leads to life; the gain of the wicked to sin.

Genesis 31:41 **For twenty years in your household I served you—fourteen years for your two daughters and six years for your flocks—and you have changed my wages ten times!** Most of us have all worked for an unscrupulous Laban at one time or another in our lives. Many of us have been manipulated, mistreated, and taken for granted by an employer, leader, or boss who didn't care about our well being.

In the above scripture, Jacob was fed up with being duped and mistreated for twenty years by his father-in-law Laban. Jacob was voicing his case in front of Laban and God. He had labored during the very hot days and the bone-chilling nights, plus the constant pressure to produce wealth for his ungrateful father-in-law. Jacob had hit the proverbial wall, and enough was enough.

The fact that we can all relate to Jacob in this

situation should give us pause. Why are we so quick to gather our forces to deal with a bully and a Laban type spirit when it is prevalent in the everyday workplace? Yet, we put up with the attacks of the enemy when it concerns our soul. This Laban craftiness and ripoff approach is the same attitude the devil uses on us in the spirit realm. When are we going to shout? "Enough is enough, I rebuke you, devil, in the name of Jesus!" Matt. 4:10a **Then Jesus told him, "Go away, Satan!**

I once worked for an owner-manager of a company who had this same Laban spirit. He changed my method of remuneration three times in three years. He kept changing the program to suit his fiscal advantage. Work became hard to accomplish anything of worth because the pay structure could not be trusted. If it hadn't been for God's favor in my life during those hard days, I would not have prospered. The day came when I had to say, "Enough is enough. Time to move on."

The Lord led me toward better prospects in life, work, and ministry. Prov. 10:16a **The wage of the righteous leads to life.** I learned how to hear what God was saying to my heart, rather than listening to the crafty speeches Laban was using. Isa.30:21 **And whenever you turn to the right or to the left, your ears will hear this command behind you: "This is the way. Walk-in it."**

So many people think they are stuck in a dead-end job, life, or career with no future. They wrongly believe that no one knows they exist and that God does not even care whether they make it or not. This is so far from the truth. They have been listening to Laban's voice for so long that they have become tone-deaf to the voice of possibilities. With God, all things are possible!

The devil will lie and steal our dreams and visions. A liar will always lie and will blind many with tricks and traps. 2Cor. 4:4 **In their case, the god of this age has blinded the minds of the unbelievers to keep them from seeing the light of the gospel of the glory of Christ, who is the image of God.** If we would just turn our eyes upon Jesus, then the bright light of truth would break through the bold-faced lies being told twenty-four-seven by the enemy of our soul.

Jesus came to break us free from the vice-grips of poverty, sickness, and spiritual death.

We do not have to work for our salvation as the devil would have us believe. Salvation is a gift from God, the Father, for those who would receive Jesus as Lord. Grace upon grace has been lavished on us, and the love of God overflows toward us continually. If God freely gave Jesus to us, will He not give us all the grace we need to have victory in life? Rom. 8:32 **Since he did not spare even his own Son but gave him up for us all, won't he also give us everything else?**

The Lord has broken the spirit of Laban's ruthlessness over our lives. The devil has no authority, hold, or legal right to our lives. We have been bought and paid for in full with the blood of Jesus. Leave the dead-end thinking that can happen when working under Laban's labor laws. It is time to shout, "Enough is enough, I am a child of God, and I am fully loved by my heavenly Father. In the Lord's presence, is where I live, work, and play." Acts 17:28a **For in him we live and move and have our being.** Blessings and peace be on us all.

HEALING OF THE MEMORIES

Proverbs 10:7 We have happy memories of the godly, but the name of a wicked person rots away.

Quote, Carl Jung: "I am not what happened to me. I am what I choose to become."

She said, "I don't like talking about that, it brings up painful memories, but I want to be healed of my anxiety." I said, "You can't fix what you will not admit needs fixing." There it is saints, a battle that so many people are fighting and getting nowhere because of their strategy - I don't want to think about it!

If the memories of your past are not affecting your ability to function, and you feel things are copacetic, then move on and give life the best you can. However, if your memories are haunting you and causing anxious apprehension, which hinders your ability to move forward, then you have to confront that ever-present issue. How are we going to get healed of our past anguishing sore spots that keep showing up if we do not confront them and bring an end to their painful effects?

When a traumatic memory continually finds its way into our thoughts, then it is time to deal with and forgive the root reason that causes the reoccurring pain. In most cases, we will have to forgive those who did hurt us regardless of how awful the atrocity was, and we might have to also forgive ourselves as much as the others who were involved in causing the hurts that keep resurfacing. Forgiving ourselves is a hard row to hoe. We can be merciless with ourselves and more judgmental than Satan. The problem with this kind of self-punishment is that we end up giving the enemy of our soul ammunition to beat us up with while crying out to God for help. How neurotic is that?

Once the Holy Spirit prompts a person to acknowledge the hurts of their past, they would be wise to allow God to heal the emotional wounds that person carries. I remember the process I went through when God started nudging me toward forgiving my father for all the evil that he lashed out on my mother, siblings, and myself. It took a few years from the first promptings of the Holy Spirit until I was clear in my intentions to fully forgive my father. Through Christ, the Lord, and by faith, I finally received the healing that was given to me at the cross, and broke the shackles that bound my heart because of the anger and unforgiveness that was living there. The liberation and feelings of peace that filled all areas of my life, could not be adequately expressed or explained. All I can say is that when I forgave my father, I received my healing. Prov. 10:7a **We have happy memories of the godly.** Was it easy? No, but for me, it was necessary.

We have to realize that when the Lord is prompting our hearts to reason with Him and become healed from our painful memories, there is no better time to do it. God is leading the healing process and He will guide us through all that is needed to be done in the right way, even if it seems difficult to us. The Lord can be trusted not to betray our exposed souls and raw emotions because His intentions for our lives are always from His heart of affectionate love. Sng. 2:4b **And his banner over me was love.** God wants us healed and living in His peace.

There is an epidemic of mental pain and hurts throughout the world and it is just as prevalent in the church. The latest statistics of people who are looking for help because of anxiety, depression, loneliness, and mental disorders of every kind have exploded, and the services available to the public cannot tackle the backlog of people screaming for help. Is it any wonder the number of psychopathic eruptions throughout all aspects of life and locations is manifesting in such irrational behaviour? People who are at the end of their rope, are lashing out with whatever weapon is in arm's reach and destroying anything and anyone in front of them. This is madness gone to seed, because of the raging pain within.

It is easy to dispense advice and say one should be healed but how does a person go about it? I have counselled people in this area, and I have found a few methods that have worked and helped people take the step of faith toward their healing. For me, my step of faith in becoming healed was to write the whole story down on paper, leaving none of the gory details out. The words written came out in fits of anger and spewed expletives, and that was the way it was. The act of describing the events that caused my deep wounds was a tumultuous and teary experience, but still an act of faith. I noticed that once all the horrific events were written down on paper, it seemed easier to voice my words of forgiveness toward my father. Once fully written, I tossed the stack of papers containing the vile story on the table, and as the collated papers slid along the tabletop, so did all the pain that was once in my heart. The old hurting memories were now in the pages that lay on the table and I could see that all the mess described was over there on the tabletop and no longer within me. Hallelujah, there is power in the name of Jesus, who heals all wounds when we call upon His name by faith for our healing.

I shared this method with someone who did the same as I did, but he took the process a step further. Not only did he write the whole sordid mess out with snot and tears staining the pages, (I didn't say this was going to be pretty) he then burned the pages as a symbol that his past life was now in ashes and he could rise out of the ashes whole and healed. I have also found that using a confessor who is a trusted friend, minister, or counsellor to spill your guts out and describe the whole pustulent mess in the full vernacular of expression, is also a step of faith forward toward confronting all the structures, devils, and people who were responsible for the past pains and traumas a person may be living with.

It is a strange dichotomy that some people can live through the most horrific events and move on without letting anything bother them. Then, there are so many who cannot move forward without voicing a roaring scream that can be heard in a distant galaxy because they are containers of torment. The enemy of our soul is working hard to make sure people remember their past pains while also impressing upon people's hearts to become unreceptive to the idea of forgiving the past that hurts so much. Satan puts in overtime, influencing people to focus on the agonies of the past and the fears of the future so that they do not live a victorious life in the present. The devil maneuvers people into a place where they are torn apart by two opposites of past and future, keeping them unstable in their thoughts and feelings. Their lives become a wasteland and their ability to live stagnates.

We cannot be slothful in this area of our lives when it is time to confront the burdens of past hurts. Otherwise, our lives will be a mess of thorns. weeds, and broken walls forever in need of repair. Prov. 24:30 **I went by the field**

of the lazy man, and by the vineyard of the man devoid of understanding; 31 and there it was, all overgrown with thorns; its surface was covered with nettles; its stone wall was broken down. Why would anyone want to live that way if they do not have to? The healing of the memories is possible, but you have to want to do it. May God's healing hand be on us all, in Jesus name.

PART 1:

QUESTIONS FOR UNDERSTANDING

1. *What did you learn in this section of the book?*
2. *What surprised you the most?*
3. *What subject(s) spoke to your heart?*
4. *Did the material that you read help you understand the subject(s) more or less?*
5. *What topics are important to you? Why?*
6. *How do these articles relate to you?*
7. *After reading this section of the book, what will you change in your life?*

PART TWO:

MAKE BETTER CHOICES

Drowning In Memories

We are confronted with having to make choices every day. Learn from the choices that were made, and as we grow in our walk with the Lord, make better choices. Col. 3:23 Whatever you do, do it from the heart, as something done for the Lord and not for people.

SINNERS WANTED, APPLY WITHIN

Proverbs 1:10 My son, if sinners entice you, don't be persuaded.

Jesus said in Luke 5:32 **I have not come to call the righteous, but sinners to repentance.** Our Lord Jesus is looking for sinners and wants all the sinners He can find to apply within the finished work of the cross, where Christ's blood sacrifice has been given for every sinner to be washed of their sins. Applications for this cleansing gift of grace that cleans one's soul is a simple but crucial act of faith. All a sinner has to do is admit they are a sinner, and receive Jesus as their personal Lord. Applications are open to anyone. John 3:16 **For God loved the world so much that he gave his one and only Son, so that everyone who believes in him will not perish but have eternal life.**

If you are a sinner or have ever transgressed God's laws throughout your life, you are welcome to come before God the Father by accepting the blood sacrifice that Jesus gave of Himself through the crucifixion on the cross. This sacrificial gift covers everyone's shame, hurts, lusts, and evil past or present life. Just apply within the grace of our Lord's forgiveness. Eph. 2:8 **God saved you by his grace when you believed. And you can't take credit for this; it is a gift from God.**

Sometimes it is hard for churched people to welcome sinners into their assemblies of worship. Sinners do not feel welcome in church, and yet Jesus who is the head of the church invites sinners of every kind to come and join His family of brothers and sisters in Christ. Matt. 11:28 **Then Jesus said, "Come to me, all of you who are weary and carry heavy burdens, and I will give you rest.** Churched people often forget where they were when Jesus found them eternally lost and bound.

I remember a dipsomaniac whose struggles with alcohol were known in the community, but he came to church regularly. At one evening service, he came in late and made his way to the front seats with his pants lowered to reveal a lot of his backside while stumbling, and bouncing off of parishioners as he made his way up the center aisle looking for a seat. Gasps could be heard, with looks of indignation expressed, and judgmental smarmy snickering was being exchanged amongst the faithful. I then heard a still small voice from within my spirit say, "The difference between him and the people here, is that their addictions and sins are well hidden and not on full display the way this man's addiction is clearly seen. In some cases, they are just as stumbling drunk, dishevelled, and weak-kneed in their daily lives as this lonely intoxicated soul is. What everyone needs to know is that I love him just as I love everyone in this building." A lesson I will never forget.

The church is only as mature as much as we are mature and loving within our relationship with Christ. We tend to advertise Christian freedom while wearing a denominational straitjacket. I'm not saying to let any unruliness take over the assembling of the saints, but remember, sinners who show up at church looking for redemption and real love will not know all the rules of the recorded agreements and statements of faith that were voted upon at the denominational headquarters. Voicing our self-righteous indignation at the young man wearing a Megadeth T-shirt who showed up at a church service because he was invited to come and see what the Lord is doing in people's lives - would not be a righteous hand of invitation. He might not see the genuine love of God he is looking for if he is judged at the door with looks of disapproval. Don't forget, you used to wear those ugly paisley ties with a polyester shirt to church meetings, and no one crucified you.

The Apostle Paul, who claimed to have been the worst sinner, made it clear in his epistles that Christ came to save sinners. 1Tim. 1:15 **Here is a trustworthy saying that deserves full acceptance: Christ Jesus came into the world to save sinners—of whom I am the worst.** Like Paul, we can all lay claim to being the worst sinner because sin is sin. What really matters is that we stop sinning. Prov. 1:10 **My son, if sinners entice you, don't be persuaded.** The sinful nature that was once predominant in our souls has been replaced with a new life in Christ, and the Lord's righteousness is now available for us to walk in for the rest of our eternal lives. 2Cor. 5:21 **For God made Christ, who never sinned, to be the offering for our sin, so that we could** be made right with God through Christ.

Ex. 17:1a **The entire Israelite community left the Wilderness of Sin, moving from one place to the next according to the LORD's command.** I don't know if this scripture was meant to be a play on words but nonetheless, good advice. Leave the *Wilderness of Sin* and follow God. At one time, we were all sinners who came to Jesus through an invitation from the Holy Spirit. *Lost Sinner* was stamped upon our hearts. All we could do was look to Jesus and receive the grace and gift of salvation He gave us by faith in His cleansing blood. The only qualification we had for His grace was that we were sin-stained and lost. As I walked up the center aisle towards the throne of God's grace, I was also dishevelled, weak-kneed, and stumbling in sin, but my application for eternal life was granted by God's merciful love. Thank you, Lord, for loving me. Amen!

ATTEMPTING FATE OR FAITH?

Proverbs 12:15 Fools think their own way is right, but the wise listen to others.

Well, I've tried everything. I guess it might be time to try God and that faith stuff. I tried it once before and not much came of it. I even put a dollar in the plate and no voice from heaven thanked me. Maybe I'll just try it again and see if two times is the charm. Who knows, that might be the way to get what I want. After all, I am enlightened and sensitive to spiritual things. 2Tim. 3:7 **Ever learning, and never able to come to the knowledge of the truth.**

There is a difference between tempting fate and believing by faith. To tempt fate or providence is not really reaching out to God. It is simply throwing a coin over your shoulder into a fountain, hoping for some conjured wish to come true. God is not some talisman you rub then repeat something you're wishing for three times and voila - there it is.

Can God meet a person who is truly looking

for Him through these worldly ways because of a lack of intimate knowledge? Sure He can, because God is so loving and will meet people where they are at when their hearts are sincere. However, God is looking for a personal relationship with His created beings and not just a Deity who is a dispenser of every type of whim and fancy.

Can someone's young son or daughter walk up to someone else's dad whom they have not known or met and say, "Hey, can you please give me a thousand dollars so I can buy a bicycle?" Sure, they could ask, but most likely there will not be the desired result because they do not know the person they are asking from and have no relationship with that person. Now God is much more sovereign than people are and answers prayers of every kind, but relationship through faith is what will grant you an everlasting blessing of life and fulfillment. Heb. 11:6 **But without faith it is impossible to please him: for he that comes to God must believe that he is, and that he is a rewarder of them that diligently seek him.**

Jesus said in effect, "If you know me you have met God the Father. John 14:7 **If you know me,**

you will also know my Father. From now on you do know him and have seen him. We see it over and over again in the Gospels that anyone who had a true encounter with Jesus - no matter how bad their lives had been - would immediately want more of Jesus.

The Lord inspired relationship and genuine accountability to God after the realization of the love God had toward them. The reality of faith was stirred up in these people's hearts and no longer was there a need for fatalism to determine their life's future. Faith had been manifested within their souls and could now help discern their lives.

The list of people who once walked at tempting fate now moved throughout the kingdom of God by faith. The demon possessed man of Gadara went from madness and insanity to wanting to follow Jesus in his healed and right mind. Zacchaeus, the dishonest tax collector, went from being a miser to an open-hearted man of generosity after encountering the love and conviction of Jesus.

Mary Magdalene, of whom Jesus cast out seven devils, followed and worked with the disciples throughout Jesus' ministry because of the dignity Jesus gave her through the love of God. The woman at the well who could not keep a relationship with any of the six men she had lived with could now permanently be in a loving relationship with God. When people met Jesus with their hearts - their hearts were changed.

The Apostle Paul, after years of walking and ministering the good news of Jesus Christ, found himself only wanting more of Jesus. Phil. 3:10a **I want to know Christ and experience the mighty power that raised him from the dead.** It is living by faith that a relationship with God is developed. Tempting fate is not conducive to a fulfilled life, but rather putting our faith in the one who gave His life for us is the way to a relationship with the only wise and loving heavenly Father.

People can either put their trust in worldly providence or substantial faith. As for me and my life, I choose faith in Christ because that gives me a relationship with God the Father. Psalm 20:7 **Some trust in chariots and others in horses, but we trust in the name of the LORD our God.**

SOMEONE SHOULD DO SOMETHING

Proverbs 21:1 The king's heart is in the hand of the LORD, as the rivers of water: He turns it wherever He will.

How often have we heard someone blurt out this statement? "Someone should do something!" Well, my friends, that someone is you and me. We are the hands extended in this earth to whom God has given His mandate. We are the salt and blessing to this fractured world.

One of the last instructions Jesus gave us before He ascended was to go into this fallen world and proclaim that there is some good news for all creation. Mark 16:15 **And he said to them, "Go into all the world and proclaim the gospel to the whole creation.**

We often dismiss ourselves from the ones who are to go into the world because we do not think or believe we are qualified or called to extend the grace of God toward the needs in this world. That is one of the biggest lies Satan has sown on this earth.

If you have genuinely received Jesus Christ into your heart as your savior then you are more than qualified to give an account or reason for the joy, peace, or change in your life. 1Pet. 3:15 **But in your hearts revere Christ as Lord. Always be prepared to give an answer to everyone who asks you to give the reason for the hope that you have. But do this with gentleness and respect.**

The Lord uses weak things or even foolish things as perceived by man to determine the destiny of mankind. 1Cor. 1:27 **But God chose the foolish things of the world to shame the wise; God chose the weak things of the world to shame the strong.** God is not saying that He has a monopoly on foolishness or only the ignorance of man is available to Him, but rather He can use whoever and whatever He wants to get His wisdom across into our heart. Prov. 21:1 **The king's heart is in the hand of the LORD, as the rivers of water: he turns it wherever he will.**

We are the whoever or the someone who should do something to help in the difficult situations of life. We are a walking Gospel of God

in this hurt and desperate world. In most cases for a lot of people that we come across in our daily walk, we are the only Bible they will ever get to read. We are read and even judged daily as we express the heart of God toward mankind. 2Cor. 3:2 **Ye are our epistle written in our hearts, known and read of all men.**

We just have to look through the bible to see that God uses ordinary people to do extraordinary things in and for the kingdom of God. We read about Deborah who judged Israel and was described as a mother in Israel. Jud. 5:7 **There were few people left in the villages of Israel--until Deborah arose as a mother for Israel.**

God used Jephthah, a social outcast, to deliver Israel. Jud. 11:2 **Gilead's wife also had several sons, and when these half brothers grew up, they chased Jephthah off the land. "You will not get any of our father's inheritance," they said, "for you are the son of a prostitute."** The prophet Amos was a herdsman. Amos 1:1a **The words of Amos, who was among the herdsmen of Tekoa.**

The Apostle Peter was a fisherman. Matthew was a tax collector. The Apostle Paul worked with

Aquila and Priscilla who were tentmakers but influenced the movement of the Gospel of Jesus Christ. Acts 18:3 **And because he was of the same trade he stayed with them and worked, for they were tentmakers by trade.**

Many people say, "I am just a laborer or a mechanic or a store clerk and so on." No, saints. You are the someone who should do something about what you are seeing that is disturbing your heart. The Lord has allowed that irritation to bother you so you can step up to the plate with God's direction and blessing to do something about it. Don't just curse the darkness, but rather, bring light to the situation.

You are the light of the world and yes, there may be some opposition to what God has put in your heart to do. However, you and God are a majority. Church history shows us that we have the right and freedom today of owning and reading the Bible. This came at a great cost to many who forfeited their very lives to get that privilege for us.

God can turn the heart of anyone in opposition to His plan that He is using you in. Before you say, "Someone should do something," ask yourself what you can do about the situation. You may be the one with the answer. Esther 4:14b **And who knows whether thou art come to the kingdom for such a time as this?** May God give us the wisdom and courage to step up and be that someone.

SORRY TO INFORM YOU

Proverbs 21:2 A person may think their own ways are right, but the LORD weighs the heart.

Japanese Proverb: If you understand everything, you must be misinformed.

How has it become possible that so many people are absolute authorities on everything and anything ever said, done, or invented throughout the history of this world? Just wondering because I am still learning so many of the mysteries that life has to offer. It must be dismal for countless individuals to have reached the pinnacle of all knowledge and know that there is nothing left to learn or experience in life because they know all that is knowable. This may come as a shock to some of you, but, I am sorry to inform you that you have been taking yourself way too seriously lately. We need to get healed from the inflated egos that are now the default setting in many of our lives.

We have to start learning how to laugh at ourselves again. Prov. 17:22a **A merry heart**

doeth good like a medicine. Getting rid of the hyper seriousness that has lodged within our self-awareness would be a good place to start humbling ourselves so that God can get through to our hearts. Prov. 21:2 **A person may think their own ways are right, but the LORD weighs the heart.** To become an authority on anything takes a lifetime of intense learning, and even then, there is still vast amounts to learn. We may have a lot of information about a particular subject and have been involved in that field our whole lives, but there is more to learn.

Ugh, especially lately, when someone says, "I have done the research, and I have all the information on that subject," I cringe inside because their foundations of fact-finding are already yesterday's news and those facts have become challengeable with new findings. At this point, I think about their spoken claim, "I did all the research" and think, "Everything they are about to say is true, except for the parts that aren't." Life, news, and times are ever-evolving and new information is forever coming forth. I am sorry to inform you, that we will never know all that is knowable even if we are convinced we do.

I realize that a lot of people are finally coming out of the lengthy restrictions and lockdowns that have quelled the hearts and emotions of many. These same people are ready to explode with a lot of things to say, but please have some thought before you say what cannot be taken back after it is said. We will be judged for our spoken unbridled opinions, and we will have to make an account before God of our idle and empty words. Matt. 12:36 **But I tell you that everyone will have to give account on the day of judgment for every empty word they have spoken.** Ouch! This scripture has always convicted me because I talk a lot. Oh, grace oh grace pour out on me!

The only truth that does not change is the love God has for us and His righteousness that has been given to us through Christ. Mal. 3:6a **For I am the LORD, I change not.** Even then, we are the ones who are changing within our relationship with our Lord. The Lord's eternal hope is working within us and is maturing our spiritual growth in His righteousness because His all-knowing presence is alive within us. The wisdom we might want to adopt is to take the grace God has given us and put our full strength into acknowledging the only all-knowing God so that when we need to know the truth of a matter, we have the loving source of all knowledge helping us understand. Psalm 139:2 **You know when I sit down or stand up. You know my thoughts even when I'm far away.**

Like so many people coming out from under a funk and fog of long-term memory loss, I too have to recognize that not all is well with everyone. We will all need a time of healing and grace for each other to find our way back to a semblance of normality - if there is such a thing. Only God has the all-knowing answers to what is needed right now. Only the Lord has the rest we are looking for. It is in Christ that we live and have our being. I am sorry to inform you that you do not have all the answers to your life, even if you think you do. No, we do not know all that is knowable, but Jesus, our Saviour does. God bless and help us all.

OUR CREDIBILITY IS WANING

Proverbs 22:1 A good name is more desirable than great riches; to be esteemed is better than silver or gold.

Our credibility will become real to ourselves when we stop borrowing the credibility of others or using high-end stuff, such as (cars, portfolios, and properties) to define who we are. Take away the possessions of a person and what remains is the real person. We do not have to borrow or steal the status of others to be affirmed in this life when we have the Lord's assurance of His love abiding within us. Our standing in the Lord is based on what God says is true and what righteousness is in Christ, and not what we mistakenly think it might be. Righteousness, integrity, and credibility in Christ are what God proclaims these virtues to be.

At times, some Christians presume to have spiritual credibility by trying to make God say something He did not say or even meant to be implied. They sometimes mix their faith and the spurious correlations of their syncretistic beliefs into a form of personal dogma, creating an illusion of credibility. These polymorphic views are manifesting in church circles because of undisciplined lifestyles, uncontrolled emotions, and their adopted soulism that leads them into carnal choices rather than being changed from glory to glory by the conviction of God's word that leads believers into righteous living.

The upshot with this loose method of belief is that any hair-raising or goosebump sensation these people experience will become their divine guidance system to their high-minded spirituality, when in fact, their soul is now in a position to be self-deceived by any bump in the night noise. The credibility they thought they borrowed from God's word to falsify their personal value and fabricated doctrine, ends up judging their immature faith. By claiming to be more open to the ways of God, they end up closed to the Lord's conviction of true righteousness that validates our eternal lives in Christ. 1Tim. 6:20 **Timothy, guard what God has entrusted to you. Avoid godless, foolish discussions with those who oppose you with their so-called knowledge.**

We see what happens when credibility and integrity are borrowed rather than lived and grown into. Samuel's two sons had corrupted the priesthood that came to them through nepotism. Samuel was a man of God who lived by faith, and all of Samuel's prophecies came true. 1Sam. 3:19 **So Samuel grew, and the LORD was with him and let none of his words fall to the ground.** Samuel was a loved Judge of Israel. His sons took over the responsibility for the nation's spiritual well-being. The problem was that Samuel's sons Joel and Abiah were corrupt, and the only reason they were in control of judging Israel and the priesthood was that they got the job by default. The little credibility these young men had, was the credibility and integrity that Samuel had walked in his whole life.

Joel and Abiah had no integral heart for God to minister the way God wanted the priesthood to work. Pretending to have a form of Godliness because of the priestly office they held and the garments they wore, did not hide the reality that they only wanted the money and power that came with the position. 1Sam. 8:3 **But they were not like their father, for they were greedy for**

money. They accepted bribes and perverted justice. The sad thing is that these (I'll do religion my way) sons had corrupted the priesthood to the point that the people of Israel felt better off with a worldly governmental system rather than what God had set up for them to remain free people. 1Sam. 8:5 **They said to him, "You are old, and your sons do not follow your ways; now appoint a king to lead us, such as all the other nations have."**

Without the Lord's righteousness at work within our souls, our credibility and integrity are only as strong as we are in the flesh. Whereas, when we are walking in the Lord's salvation we have the leading of the Holy Spirit to strengthen our resolve to choose God's righteousness rather than our own. By faith, we have the strength to make the harder choices that have to be made because the integrity of God is at work within us to help us make the hard decisions our flesh does not want to make. To stop our credibility from waning, we will have to keep choosing Christ's righteousness and not our version of it. Prov. 22:1a **A good name is more desirable than great riches.** We will have to depend on more than our good name to be in right standing with our Heavenly Father. We will have to be saved in the name that is above every name Jesus our Lord. Blessings and peace be on us all.

I QUIT!

Proverbs 4:25 Let your eyes look straight ahead; fix your gaze directly before you.

"That's it, I quit. I'm done, count me out. It's over, I'm finished with the ministry," The minister wanted to say out loud, but couldn't because the question awaiting him just hung there, like a church bell ready to be rung. "What are you going to do once you shut it down?" came the question to his mind. "Oh, something or other," he said. Therein is the dilemma. What are you going to do with the calling upon your life? The Apostle Peter had to answer this question after the Lord had been crucified. Not sure what was coming next, Peter went back to fishing. John 21:3a **Simon Peter said, "I'm going fishing."** Not a bad idea. Just shut it down, and go fishing. Then what?

I believe I am describing what a lot of men and women who are in church ministry contend with, as some have tried to quit and get out of ministerial responsibility, serving the poor who will always be with us, and enduring the sometimes laboriousness of church life. These worn-out ministers find themselves in a confused and wearisome situation while having deep inner questions to answer that are running at lightning speed through their minds. "What next? How do I turn off the conviction of my heart concerning the calling of God? What would I do, and if I find something to do, how do I go about it? Will God support my decision?" Rom. 7:24a **Oh, what a miserable person I am!** I feel miserable for staying and damned for quitting. What do I do with these thoughts? "Help me, Lord," becomes the constant prayer of desperation.

Jeremiah found himself in a similar situation. He had become disheartened with prophesying what God had put in his heart because the result of saying what God had spoken was constant persecution against himself. He was lowered into the bottom of a well for being forthright. Jer. 38:6a **So the officials took Jeremiah from his cell and lowered him by ropes into an empty cistern in the prison yard.** He was feeling the pressure of being whipped, then bound with stocks. Jer. 20:2 **So he arrested Jeremiah the prophet and**

had him whipped and put in stocks at the Benjamin Gate of the LORD's Temple. The suffering that Jeremiah went through because of the calling that had been placed upon his life at birth, had become burdensome to live with.

Jeremiah wanted to quit the whole thing but ended up saying he had an inner compelling desire to speak because God's word burned in his bones. Jer. 20:9 **But if I say, "I will not mention His word or speak anymore in His name," His word is in my heart like a fire, a fire shut up in my bones. I am weary of holding it in; indeed, I cannot.** He admits, "Yes, indeed I cannot hold back the anointed unction of God's living word." The word of the Lord lives and moves, for it will do what God says the word will do. Isa. 55:11 **So is my word that goes out from my mouth: It will not return to me empty, but will accomplish what I desire and achieve the purpose for which I sent it.**

Some may sense the assignment God has given them to be too hard to bear, and like Jonah, they want to quit the assignment they have been given. As Jonah did, they run away as far as possible from God. Not a good plan or even possible since God is everywhere. Jonah wanted out of the responsibility of the ministry assignment he was to bring to Nineveh. However, after he had reluctantly agreed to go to Nineveh and prophecy about what he was supposed to proclaim, again Jonah wants to quit, but this time, on his own life. Jonah 4:3 **Now, LORD, take away my life, for it is better for me to die than to live.** We can end up tired of everything churchy and ministerial if we are not close to the heart of God. We can find ourselves put out, burned out, and fed up with what we perceive to be unthankful people and the toil of ministry work. Becoming bitter rather than better, we end up on the slag-heap of washed-up ministers gasping for a breath of holy air.

Elijah, with God's clear directions, had pulled off one of the greatest feats on Mount Carmel by calling down fire from heaven to consume everything on the altar and consume the altar itself. One would think Elijah had it all together and possessed an arsenal of ministerial weapons at his disposal. Yet, after his incredible victory over the four hundred priests of Baal, when threatened by Jezebel, he runs away wanting to give up and die. 1Kings 19:4 **Then he went on alone into the wilderness, traveling all day. He sat down under a solitary broom tree and prayed that he might die. "I have had enough, LORD," he said. "Take my life, for I am no better than my ancestors who have already died."**

We need God at all times, especially when we want to give up. The Lord has the answers, and He will continue to give them to us if we ask by faith. James 1:5 **If you need wisdom, ask our generous God, and he will give it to you. He will not rebuke you for asking.** If we are going to give up, then let us quit believing the enemy of our soul who lies all the time. If we are going to quit, then let us quit doubting God and doubting His love for us.

Father, in Jesus name, Help us ask you for help when we feel overwhelmed and want to shut down. Lord, fix our hearts with grace and your courage, so we can prevail when the desire to give up is the strongest. Prov. 4:25 **Let your eyes look straight ahead; fix your gaze directly before you.** May God's face shine on all the ministers who are sowing God's love into our lives. We look to Jesus who did not quit while on His way to the cross to die for us all. Amen!

SOUR GRAPES

Proverbs 20:14 "It's no good, it's no good!" says the buyer— then goes off and boasts about the purchase.

Why am I not being blessed like brother Barry? Doesn't God know I needed that blessing more than he did? Why did God give that house to that family and not us? I have been begging God for a house for our family. Why did Mary get that job and I didn't? Surely God knows Mary has more money than I do. Why don't I get the blessings I need and everyone else is getting theirs? Why did Carolyn get healed? She only goes to church once a month. I go every Sunday and I'm still sick.

It almost sounds petulant and childish when hearing these complaints but nonetheless, they are voiced every day by God-fearing people who are stuck in the frustration of their faith. God's answer to all these sour grape prayers is get the covetousness out of our talk and start believing God for real answers to faith-filled prayer. Heb. 13:5 **Let your conversation be**

without covetousness; and be content with such things as ye have: for he hath said, I will never leave thee, nor forsake thee. Saints, this life is not a reality show; it is reality.

We live in a braggadocious and a one-up society where scamming and getting popular because of the art of that particular scam is applauded. This type of acceptable living is becoming our morning water-cooler or coffee-bar talk and viewing pleasure. The more outrageous and belligerent the act is, the faster it becomes available to viewers on a variety of social apps available to the whole world.

Popularity by clicks and bites does not necessarily create an honest character. Some people think we can bring this fame and notoriety found on the world's social media platform to the throne room of God and get special treatment. "Hey God! I have five hundred friends on this page and I need your blessing to improve my social status." Prayer without faith can become redundant and the result is often a great big silence from heaven resulting in a sour grape attitude toward God and church. Prov. 19:3 **The stupidity of a person turns his life upside**

down, and his heart rages against the LORD.

We need to learn how to rejoice in the blessing and prosperity of others without feeling we will be left out of God's plan. We should not be comparing ourselves with others in the quantity of stuff attained in life or even ministries that have grown in the favor of God. Stop worrying about what you think people are getting away with. Psalm 37:7 **Be still before the LORD and wait patiently for him; do not fret when people succeed in their ways, when they carry out their wicked schemes.**

I like what Gloria Copeland says when she sees others being blessed. She says, "Praise the Lord, the line is moving and my turn should be coming up soon." No sour grapes there. She has learned to rejoice in the prosperity of others and we need this ability in our lives also. When our attitude is to help people get what they want in life, it will not be long before we get what we want for our lives. God is just and has put desires into our hearts. Psalm 20:4 **May he give you the desire of your heart and make all your plans succeed.** It is His good pleasure to give us His kingdom and the abilities to work within it. Luke 12:32 **Fear**

not, little flock, for it is your Father's good pleasure to give you the kingdom.

There is no need to live in fear of being left out or having to resort to a schemer's way of life to get by. We do not have to become so cunning as to trick people out of their livelihood to get ahead. Prov. 20:14 **"It's no good, it's no good!" says the buyer-- then goes off and boasts about the purchase.** Our God is a giving God and asks that we come to Him in faith, asking for what we need to live and also grow in the dreams God has put within our hearts. God is not trying to take away our reason for existing; He is trying to help us grow and mature so we can fulfill our reason for living in Christ.

There are no reasons for sour grapes in our lives when we approach God under His terms. The Lord is not impressed with our charisma or social standing. He is interested in our character of heart and love for His will in our lives. Don't try to put your best foot forward. God already knows you too well and all your secrets. Just be you. Let us grow and mature in the love of God and not become infantile complainers, turning every event into a sour grape catastrophe because we did not get our way. Let us trust God and his thoughts toward us. He knows who we are and what we need. Jer. 29:11 **For I know the plans I have for you," declares the LORD, "plans to prosper you and not to harm you, plans to give you hope and a future.**

THROWING GOD UNDER THE BUS

Proverbs 19:3 A man's own folly subverts his way, yet his heart rages against the LORD.

To throw someone under the bus is an idiomatic phrase in American English meaning to betray a friend or ally for selfish reasons.

I once used this phrase while talking to God when I casually said, "Hey God! I feel like you are throwing me under the bus here." Then the realization set into my mind and heart that it is impossible for God to betray me for selfish reasons. If anything, I was the one throwing God under the bus because of my obvious immaturity in what I was saying. James 1:13 **When tempted, no one should say, "God is tempting me." For God cannot be tempted by evil, nor does He tempt anyone.**

How often do we blame God for all the misfortunes that happen to us? We rage against God while running amok in our attempts to be the god of our own life. Prov. 19:3 **A man's own folly subverts his way, yet his heart rages**

against the LORD. When do we finally realize that God is trying to save us from ourselves and a Christless eternity? When we become deceived into believing God is the problem in our life, we have elevated ourselves above the greatness of God. This type of hubris can be disguised as a form of righteousness, but it ends up being self-righteousness and we throw God under the bus one more time.

Michael Horton said, "The power of God unto salvation is not our passion for God, but the passion He has exhibited toward us sinners by sending His own Son to redeem us." Rom. 1:16 **For I am not ashamed of the gospel, for it is the power of God for salvation to everyone who believes, to the Jew first and also to the Greek.** The Apostle Paul was confident in God's power of salvation through Christ because Jesus was Lord in Paul's heart and life.

If we do not remove ourselves from the throne of our own heart and place Jesus there only - then we are living and preaching a Christless Christianity. What good is a Christless Christianity but to become pseudo social workers using religious expressions in controlled sympathetic voice tones?

Until I clearly express that Jesus is Lord of my life, I will continue to blame God for all the bad choices I make. I will end up saying, "Why did you let me do that Lord? Why did you not stop me from doing this Lord?" On and on the accusations go. The human heart is utterly deceptive and will blame anyone, including God, for the woes caused by ourselves. Jer. 17:9 **The heart is deceitful above all things, and desperately wicked: who can know it?**

We seem to be incapable of fessing up and taking responsibility for our own actions. We would rather throw God under the bus than admit any wrongdoing. Rom. 7:24 **Oh, what a miserable person I am! Who will free me from this life that is dominated by sin and death?** How do I overcome this unwanted human characteristic?

Thank God for Jesus and the complete work that was done for me on and through the cross Jesus was nailed to. The accepted sacrifice and finished work that God accomplished through His Son Jesus will keep me in right standing with my heavenly Father for now and throughout eternity. The precious blood of Jesus has made it so.

I can count on God's faithfulness toward me and know deep in my heart that even though I may not be reliable or always get it right in life, God will never throw me under the bus. Jesus has made a way for me through His selfless life-giving gift to be at peace with God and myself. I receive it by faith. 2Tim. 2:13 **If we are not faithful, He will still be faithful. Christ cannot deny who he is.**

BEFORE YOU TASTE THE APPLE

Proverbs 13:16 Wise people think before they act; fools don't—and even brag about their foolishness.

Before you taste the apple, have you thought it through? It would have been nice if there had been some other person in the garden of Eden that day who would have piped-up just before Eve took a bite of the fruit and gave some to Adam. "Hey Eve, slow down a bit, have you really thought this through?"

Well, it did not happen that way. The echo of God's word was hovering in Adam and Eve's consciousness and was saying plainly not to eat the fruit from the tree of knowledge of good and evil. Gen. 2:16 **And the LORD God commanded the man, saying, Of every tree of the garden thou may freely eat: 17 but of the tree of the knowledge of good and evil, thou shalt not eat of it: for in the day that thou eat thereof thou shalt surely die.**

The Lord admonishes us to test the spirit in any situation that might be complex and to let His peace be our guide and beacon for knowing the will of God. 1John 4:1 **Beloved, do not believe every spirit, but test the spirits to see whether they are from God. For many false prophets have gone out into the world.**

Before you go ahead and taste that apple, test the result of the fallout from its fruit and let God's peace direct your path. Phil. 4:7 **And the peace of God, surpassing all understanding, will guard your hearts and your minds in Christ Jesus.**

Saying, "It seemed like a good idea at the time," just won't cut it when you are knee deep in the misery of the poor choice that was made. Prov. 13:16 **Wise people think before they act; fools don't—and even brag about their foolishness.**

Maybe sin and transgressions should come with labels that say, "Before you taste this, have you considered its effect?" Oh ya, that's right, there already is a book full of labels and directions for overcoming sin and becoming clean - the word of God. John 15:3 **Now ye are clean through the word which I have spoken unto you.**

We are living in a time of multiple views and

messages that can change on an hourly basis. The speed and volume of information coming at us in mega amounts may be overloading our senses and can make us feel traumatic and confused. More than ever we need an anchor or a solid rock in the storms of life to steady our souls. Building our lives on the rock is the first step. Matt. 7:24 **Therefore whosoever hears these sayings of mine, and does them, I will liken him unto a wise man, which built his house upon a rock.**

Jesus warned us that in the end times there would be false Christs or a lot of false beliefs. These pretenders would be responsible for all kinds of deceptions within society. Matt. 24:24 **For there shall arise false Christs, and false prophets, and shall shew great signs and wonders; insomuch that, if it were possible, they shall deceive the very elect.**

Jesus comforts us with the fact that we will be able to discern the lies of these false teachers because the Holy Spirit would guide us into truth. So before you act on something that you are not sure about, think of the words of our Lord and ask Him for direction. Prov. 3:6 **In all thy ways acknowledge him, and he shall direct thy**

paths.

Our Lord Jesus will never leave us nor forsake us. He will never lead us toward deception or sin but rather in the opposite direction to the Father's arms. He can be counted on to shepherd us throughout our life and be that still small voice that pipes-up and says, "Before you taste that apple, have you considered the word of God?" Thank you, Lord, for being there for us at all times. Deut. 31:6 **Be determined and confident. Do not be afraid of them. Your God, the LORD himself, will be with you. He will not fail you or abandon you.**

ANOTHER DISORDER

Proverbs 23:2 And put a knife to your throat if you are a man of great appetite.

I don't mean to be insensitive here, but, I did roll my eyes when I heard a doctor on a CBC radio interview say, "They were no longer calling it - alcoholism, it was now called alcohol use disorder." I can just hear the men and women who have come to terms with their alcoholism, say at the next AA meeting, "Hi my name is Norm, and I am a victim of alcohol use disorder." No! To be healed of it, you have to take responsibility for what it is - alcohol addiction and not some froo-froo disorder. Excuse my vernacular here, but before I knew the Lord as my saviour, I was a dumb-ass alcoholic drunk. I was not a witless-buttocks who had problems with alcohol use disorder. Oh please!

When are we going to man-up so to speak, and stop blaming all our problems on another new disorder? Like most of you, I have compassion for people who suffer under any oppressive addiction, because not but the grace of God, there go I. We, as a society, want answers for those who need help breaking their addictions, but as Anne Lamott says, "When are we going to stop and try to heal our sick stressed minds with our sick stressed minds?" We need real answers and not another disorder to blame our woes on. Matt. 15:14b **They are blind guides of the blind. And if a blind man guides a blind man, both will fall into a pit.**

In the late 1970s, I was an alcoholic. After finally accepting personal responsibility for my addiction to alcohol, I was able to break the habit with God's healing grace and power in my life. By God's grace, I still live in blessed sobriety to this day. Phil. 4:13 **I can do all things through Christ which strengtheneth me.** A few years ago, I helped a young man who was addicted to heroin, break free of its ruthless and merciless cravings. When he was at the nadir of his addiction, he wanted to be free, and he wanted that freedom with all his mind, heart, and soul. I'm happy to say that today, he is living a drug-free healthy life, and has become a wonderful husband and father.

One of the complaints he had at the time he was battling his drug addiction, was that the doctors who were handing out the methadone prescriptions were all too ready at the slightest hint of difficulty to raise the dosage. He said, "The doctors think they are helping by babying the addict, but they are almost guaranteeing the addict will fail in their recovery, because the doctors see them as victims, and not as people who might break through." Wow! What insight.

This young man felt he was fighting a battle on two fronts. I'm paraphrasing what he said, "I was addicted to heroin, but the doctors treated me like I was only pharmaceutically challenged. It's so hard to get out of the system of drugs, whether it is legal or illegal." I don't believe all doctors are that way. A lot of good doctors and compassionate drug counsellors are stuck within an overlegislated medical system that promotes prescriptions rather than hands-on healing. Therefore, they come out with more disorders and syndromes to try and accommodate the multitudes of hurting people looking for help. I reckon all we can say is, "Physician, heal thyself."

We live in a restless society where the appetite

for everything being sensational and extreme is also bringing with it - extreme binge drinking, heavy drug use, and many other overindulgent risky lifestyles. Prov. 23:2 **And put a knife to your throat if you are a man of great appetite.** Self-destructive behavior has almost become mainstream. The results are addictions to anything that can relieve the present pains in life. We will need more than labelling these souls as suffering a disorder. We need real power - the kind of power that God has.

When we begin to call sin what it is, and not cover it up with another catchy slogan, then, the results will be healing for the lost, addicted, and tormented. The Lord asks us to confess our sins to Him so that we may get rid of them and the deadly effects they cause. The road to recovery is asking the Lord for His powerful help. 1John 1:9 **If we confess our sins, he is faithful and just to forgive us our sins, and to cleanse us from all unrighteousness.** Grace and a clean conscience will give us the strength to kick the bad habit.

By simply calling every human difficulty a disorder, is a disservice to those who want out of their addictions. Hi, my name is Norm, and I take ownership of the decisions I have made in my life. Because of that fact, I repent of the wrongs and sins I committed throughout my life. My bad behavior was not a disease, it was sin, and I must confess it to God so that I can get rid of it.

It is the Lord who gives us the power to overcome and fight any addiction that would try to attach itself to our body and soul. 2Cor. 10:4 **The weapons we fight with are not the weapons of the world. On the contrary, they have divine power to demolish strongholds** 5 **we destroy arguments and every lofty opinion raised against the knowledge of God, and take every thought captive to obey Christ.** This is how we win. We do it with God! May God give us all the ability to overcome the battles we are going through. Amen!

PART TWO:

QUESTIONS FOR UNDERSTANDING

1. *What did you learn in this section of the book?*
2. *What surprised you the most?*
3. *What subject(s) spoke to your heart?*
4. *Did the material that you read help you understand the subject(s) more or less?*
5. *What topics are important to you? Why?*
6. *How do these articles relate to you?*
7. *After reading this section of the book, what will you change in your life?*

PART THREE:

FRUIT OF THE SPIRIT

Drowning In Memories

The fruit of the Holy Spirit is at work within our lives, and it will show who we are and who God made us to be. Let the Spirit reign that Christ may be seen by all man. Gal. 5:22 But the fruit of the Spirit is love, joy, peace, longsuffering, gentleness, goodness, faith, 23 meekness, temperance: against such there is no law.

I WAS WRONG

Proverbs 29:1 Whoever stubbornly refuses to accept criticism will suddenly be destroyed beyond recovery.

Before having a stroke, I was living a very unhealthy lifestyle that caused heart disease, which led to a stroke and all the suffering that came afterward. I had to repent and ask God for help to establish a healthier lifestyle because I was wrong in my previous health choices. I even had the nerve to question God as to why He had not warned me of the health issue - when in the middle of that very thought, God showed me that on four occasions, in four different towns, where and when He had warned me. The thing was, I did not recognize the severity of the warning. I was wrong in my estimation of the potential problem.

I had recently discovered something about a writer whose books I do not like, and I had judged the writer to be as unlikeable as his books. I came across an interview with this author and I was astounded at the amount of work he has put into helping those who cannot read and the generous donations he has given to thousands of schools, libraries, and scholarships for the advancement of literacy to help the poor and marginalized people throughout North America. I was wrong about him as a person, and I had to repent concerning my attitude toward him. I still do not like his books, but I have found a new admiration and respect for the soul and heart of this writer.

I was talking with my automotive mechanic about one of his employees whom I felt was a loser. It turns out I'm the loser for thinking it. The man in question has one of the best work ethics in that business establishment and is one of the most reliable mechanics working there. I was wrong in my judgment of his character and abilities. I had judged a man before I got to know him. Prov. 30:10 **Never slander a worker to the employer, or the person will curse you, and you will pay for it.** Again, I had to repent. We do not always get it right, but when we are wrong we should admit it, or we will be in danger of becoming destroyed beyond recovery.

The downfall of King Saul was his

stubbornness not to accept criticism when he was wrong. Saul's insecurities could not handle a rebuke from his son Jonathan or other members of his royal household concerning David's faithfulness toward the king. Prov. 29:1 **He who is often rebuked, and hardens his neck, will suddenly be destroyed, and that without remedy.** Saul was suspicious of all the people around him and accused everyone of conspiring against him. His obdurate determination to be right when he was wrong was clouding his judgment in all areas of his life.

The emotional immaturity that was influencing Saul, allowed a spirit of pride that drove Saul to madness. The oddness of this needless suffering was that he needed David to play music to help drive away the heavy spirit of depression Saul was fighting. 1Sam. 16:23b **David took a harp, and played with his hand: So Saul was refreshed, and was well, and the evil spirit departed from him.** The person Saul hated, was the one helping him through his self-made anxiety. All he had to do was admit he was wrong and act upon that fact. Saul died a jealous man believing a lie because he would not admit to being wrong.

Drowning In Memories

The pride of life can cause unnecessary problems in all aspects of relationships. 1John 2:16 **For everything in the world—the lust of the flesh, the lust of the eyes, and the pride of life—comes not from the Father but from the world.** How many marriages could have been saved had a spouse admitted to being wrong? How many partnerships could have prospered had management admitted to being wrong when the work plan was not prospering? Admitting we are wrong is a quality of heart that comes from God and places us in a position to be helped and forgiven. I've been wrong about a whole lot of things, and I am so grateful to God that He was not wrong about me. Yes, even when we are wrong, the Lord loves us and helps us make it right. Blessings.

THEN, I WOULD BE HAPPY

Proverbs 16:20 He that handles a matter wisely shall find good: and whoso trusts in the LORD, happy is he.

How elusive is the concept of happiness that lingers just outside our grasp? The idea of happiness we create in our minds can be so unattainable. How often have we heard someone say or even heard ourselves say, "If I could just have that, then I would be happy." The word of God indicates that true happiness comes when God is involved with our choices and directions we take in life. Job 5:17 **Behold, happy is the man whom God corrects: therefore despise not thou the chastening of the Almighty.**

In another place it says, Psalm 146:5 **Happy is he that has the God of Jacob for his help, whose hope is in the LORD his God.** It seems that happiness is not something we chase but rather something we possess within ourselves because God is filling us with His presence and therefore happiness comes forth out of our being.

Psalm 144:15 **Happy is that people, that is in such a case: yea, happy is that people, whose God is the LORD.**

The Apostle Paul writes in Phil. 4:11 **Not that I speak in respect of want: for I have learned, in whatsoever state I am, therewith to be content.** A few meanings of the word content are happy, at ease, fulfilled and gratified. As contentment is an acquired skill or learned as Paul expressed, so is happiness an attribute that is learned and applied to our everyday lives. We choose to have a happy heart as we grow in the favor of our God.

Waiting for happiness to fall on us like rain is a mug's game. The enemy of our soul will have us running and spending all our time and resources chasing things that will bring a temporary and watered-down version of happiness. However, within a short time after the things have been bought, charged and sometimes purloined, the novelty, shine and sparkle fade away like a dying flower.

If we look around the world, we can easily see that the devil has become effective at that part of his pathetic job. Satan tries to get people to focus on what they don't have so that they are continually in a state of unhappiness and discontentment. We need to cut the strings of that puppet scam-artist and link our hearts to the God of our salvation who is pure joy, peace and happiness. Eph. 4:27 **Neither give place to the devil.**

My favorite happy verse is Rom. 4:7 **Happy are they whose lawless acts were forgiven, and whose sins were covered.** Yes, this is true happiness. Happy is the man whose sins are forgiven, happy is that man. Well, I am that happy man. The joy, peace, and happiness that comes from a clean and clear conscience cannot be bought, purchased or charged on a credit card. It can only be realized by a heart-transforming relationship with grace through our Lord and Savior Jesus Christ.

Wow! How good is that? The mighty God who created us has made happiness a part of our inheritance when we are in a relationship with Him. No wonder the devil is hard at work in trying to distort happiness. God's form of happiness and contentment will bring peace and calm to our souls and we will be able to walk in the power and authority of God's kingdom.

If we are going to strive, then let it be for a relationship with our God who will be to us a pure contentment. If we are going to want, then let us want the fullness of the finished work of the cross in our hearts. If we are going to covet, then let us covet the gifts of the Holy Spirit that we may be the children of our God. 1Cor. 12:31 **But covet earnestly the best gifts: and yet shew I unto you a more excellent way.** If we are moved to loving something to the point of saying, "I just have to have that", then let it be the love of God within our hearts that can change the joy, peace and happiness of the whole world. Aah! Happy is the man whose sins are forgiven, happy is that man. Amen and amen!

A LOW-SIN DIET

Proverbs 5:22 An evil man is held captive by his own sins; they are ropes that catch and hold him.

Well, at least I'm not as bad as they are. I tend to cringe in my inner being when I hear the personal justification for doing something ungodly or out of God's will. Whether it comes out of my own heart or the mouth of another person, it is still wrong, wrong, wrong. How can we compare our personal self-righteousness with the personal self-righteousness of another? Whatever it is that keeps us bound to a sin cannot be alleviated by comparing ourselves to someone else who sins worse or more times than we do.

This is spiritual ignorance gone to seed. Our soul does not get brownie points for not sinning a bit less than someone else who sins. Rom. 2:21 **You therefore who are teaching others, you do not teach yourself. You who are preaching that people should not steal, you are stealing! 22 You who say that people should not commit adultery, you commit adultery, and you who**

despise idols plunder the holy place!

We must be in a state of righteousness that has been given to us through faith in the blood of Jesus and the finished work of the cross. Eph. 2:8 **For it is by grace you have been saved through faith, and this not from yourselves; it is the gift of God,** 9 **not as a result of works, so that no one may boast.**

We cannot make up our own spiritual rules as we go along to justify our own interpretation of God's word to suit what we want to do in the moment of temptation. We must overcome through grace and faith.

When we use the world's standard of ethics and social behavior as our template for righteousness, we are simply on a low-sin diet so to speak. It becomes as silly as the term "No added sugar" to the already very sweet sucrose, corn-syrup, and artificial sweetened snacks. It no longer matters that there is no added sugar to a product when the person eating it has been digesting spoonfuls of alternative sugars daily.

They may claim to be on a low-sugar diet, but we already know that strategy will go nowhere but up on the weight scale. Plus, people encounter more doctor visits for help with all the diseases that come with the high-sugar diet. As the above proverb implies, the man is held captive by his own cravings for sugar or any other vice and the ropes catch and hold him addicted to it.

A low-sin diet will have the same problem in the soul of a man when small compromises become commonplace. Like the man who has tricked himself into believing a low-sugar diet is good enough will eventually be nibbling on whatever comes his way because he has no willpower to stop.

If the word of God says not to steal, then don't steal. Stop using so much of your employer's time to catch up and answer all your social media updates. Use your own time during your own work breaks rather than steal company time. Col. 3:17 **And whatever you do, in word or deed, do it all in the name of the Lord Jesus, giving thanks to God the Father through Him.**

Someone says, "I don't understand why I cannot get victory over this repetitive sin in my life. I procrastinate, and never fulfill a promise to anyone. I spend too much money on stuff I don't need and end up short all the time owing many creditors. I waste too much time on frivolous things, ignoring the word of God. I just cannot get going in life." Well, the Lord will help you fix it with an obedient heart and a mind for God. However, you have to want it. 2Cor. 6:17 **Therefore come out from their midst and be separate, says the Lord, and touch nothing unclean, and I will receive you.**

There are no half-measures here or part-time righteous acts for living that will conquer the sins in our lives. We cannot live on or with a low-sin diet. It has to be a no-sin lifestyle. That new lifestyle can only be received through Jesus Christ the Lord and all the work He did through the cross.

Don't be fooled with alternative interpretations of what you know to be true in your own heart. If Jesus said it, then it can be counted on for eternity. John 14:6 **Jesus answered, "I am the way and the truth and the life. No one comes to the Father except through Me.** May God help us maintain a healthy spiritual and physical life. In Jesus name.

USELESS VOWS

Proverbs 20:25 It is a snare for a man to devote rashly something as holy, and afterward to reconsider his vows.

Vows, promises, and commitments are not well honored in these days of non-committal attitudes. Pay off my debt. Why? Just declare personal bankruptcy and start spending what we don't have all over again. Breaking a business deal, no problem, call a lawyer and make up some subterfuge as to why the contract is being broken.

Divorce, simple, call it quits and blame it on irreconcilable differences to sound fashionable, and we can divvy-up the kids for the weekends. Tell the truth, Bah, what's the point, they will never know they got ripped off. No harm no foul. We all got to look out for number one. Hag. 1:5 **Now therefore thus saith the LORD of hosts; Consider your ways.**

A lot of our vows and commitment to God and life itself is as reliable as a New Year's Eve resolutions; well-meaning, but absolutely without substance. What we fail to realise is that most of us will find it very difficult to follow through on anything of challenge or hardship without the help of God influencing our fortitude. John 15:5 **I am the vine, ye are the branches: He that abides in me, and I in him, the same brings forth much fruit: for without me ye can do nothing.**

We read in the story of Jonah - the shipmates find out that Jonah is the reason for the gale-force-winds that are about to sink their ship. So, the deck-hands throw Jonah overboard, as instructed, and the storm stops immediately. Jonah 1:15 **So they took up Jonah, and cast him forth into the sea: and the sea ceased from her raging.**

The next verse is the one that I find interesting because God does not respond to what is done. Jonah 1:16 **Then the men feared the LORD exceedingly, and offered a sacrifice unto the LORD, and made vows.** I would go as far as to say, "Made vows that were never honored." Vows, promises, and commitments made in the thick of major fear, anger, and desperation are most often empty promises that end up resulting in useless vows.

I say this because God does not even acknowledge anything about these vows made by the sailors. God prepares a great fish to take Jonah onward to his divine appointment in Nineveh.

There seems to be very little value that God put on these vows made from fearful hearts for self-preservation by these men. We have all heard these vows before. I promise, that was the last time I will get drunk or have a drink, it's the straight and narrow from now on. You can count on it, I will be there on time for you, and if I'm late, well, I'll make it up to you. Honest, the payment is in the mail.

Prov. 21:8 **The way of him that is laden with guilt is exceeding crooked; But as for the pure, his work is right.** The Lord has a simple solution to all this false elaboration. God says in His word. Matt. 5:37 **But let your 'Yes' be 'Yes,' and your 'No,' 'No.' For whatever is more than these is from the evil one.**

When Paul says in Phil. 4:13 **I can do all things through Christ which strengthens me,** he was also referring to the fact that he had the strength to keep his vows and promises that he made. Paul also made it clear that this ability came through Christ within and his relationship with the Lord.

We have this same Jesus living within our beings. A bit of self-diagnoses is in order and multiple trips to the counselor can be avoided if we would take a lesson from Matt. 7:16 **Ye shall know them by their fruits. Do men gather grapes of thorns, or figs of thistles?** Put the spotlight (the word of God) on our own hearts and see the fruit coming out of our lives. If the fruit is good, then praise the Lord. If not, repent. Prov. 20:11 **Even a child is known by his doings, whether his work be pure, and whether it be right.**

Keeping our vows, promises, and commitments should not be a grievous undertaking. It should be part of our born-again Christian character that is growing from glory to glory. 2Cor. 5:17 **Therefore if any man be in Christ, he is a new creature: old things are passed away; behold, all things are become new.** Being a new creature in Christ will help us live from a new spirit.

WORTHY OF ADORATION

*Proverbs 31:31 Reward her for all she has done.
Let her deeds publicly declare her praise.*

Adoration: Love and respect (someone) deeply. Worship; venerate. Psalm 95:6 **O come, let us worship and bow down: let us kneel before the LORD our maker.**

Who but Christ is worthy of adoration? The words in a praise song struck my heart this Sunday when I heard myself say with conviction, "I will adore you." Yes, that is something we can all do. We can say from our grateful hearts, "I will love and respect you Lord Jesus for who you are and for all you have done for us." With enthusiasm, I will love the Lord with all my heart, mind, strength, and soul. Psalm 18:3a **I will call upon the LORD, who is worthy to be praised.**

To adore oneself is hubris and to adore a person or an object is idolatry. Adoration is meant for God and Him alone. No one - not even an angel is worthy of God-like adoration. Satan tried to steal the praise meant for God by trafficking or taking a cut of it for himself. Eze. 28:15 **You were perfect in your ways from the day you were created, till iniquity was found in you. 16a Through your widespread trade you were filled with violence, and you sinned.**

This sinful act made Satan a corrupted, power hungry, fallen angel with egoistic and lustful cravings to the point of sinful insanity. Isa. 14:13 **For thou hast said in thine heart, I will ascend into heaven, I will exalt my throne above the stars of God: I will sit also upon the mount of the congregation, in the sides of the north: 14 I will ascend above the heights of the clouds; I will be like the most High. 15 Yet thou shalt be brought down to hell, to the sides of the pit.** What gall the devil had to think he could overpower God who created him in the first place. What a loser.

Who is worthy of adoration? Not the devil who kills, robs, and destroys, but rather God who gives life and gives it abundantly through love. The Lord saves, heals, forgives, and restores our lives with the promise of a blessed eternity, living with Him in the fullness of His love. God chose love for us even when we did not love or want Him.

Rom. 5:8 **But God demonstrates His own love toward us, in that while we were yet sinners, Christ died for us.** What more can God do for us to demonstrate His love? He chose to love us before we accepted His perfect gift - Christ crucified. Yes, He is worthy to be praised and deserves all the adoration that can ever come out of our heart.

We live in a fleeting world of frivolous stuff and ideologies. Nailing something down that has real life-giving substance is becoming difficult to find and even recognized when it does come by. God's love and promises have maintained integrity from the beginning of creation. We can count on all God has said to mankind because it is God saying it. He does not lie. 2Cor. 1:20 **For all the promises of God are "Yes" in Christ. And so through Him, our "Amen" is spoken to the glory of God.**

A soul being saved through the sacrifice of Jesus' life given on the cross is still a mighty miracle that is beyond our understanding. Only God can give us the miracle of this incredible new life in God. Your soul or my soul accepting Jesus as our Lord is an incredible miracle, because we know where we came from before we met Christ the Lord. Honesty makes us clearly say we were headed for a no win, death-ridden eternity. We were utterly lost and dead in our sins. Give Jesus the adoration due Him for all He has done for us. Lord Jesus, "I adore you and I thank you for the love you have lavished on me." Amen!

WHERE ARE THE BEREANS?

Proverbs 14:12 There is a way that seems right to a person, but its end is the way to death.

Acts 17:10 **As soon as it was night, the brothers and sisters sent Paul and Silas away to Berea. Upon arrival, they went into the synagogue of the Jews. 11 The people here were of more noble character than those in Thessalonica, since they received the word with eagerness and examined the Scriptures daily to see if these things were so.**

Just because something is said from a church pulpit, doesn't automatically mean it is true. As the Berean saints did, we should also be doing. They examined the scriptures daily to see if the things being taught were so. We are responsible for the choices we make in our Christian walk and responsible to make sure the doctrines, teachings, and ministries we are living under are biblically sound and Holy Spirit led.

Jesus said to believe in Him because of what the scriptures said. John 7:38 **He who believes**

in Me, as the Scripture has said, out of his heart will flow rivers of living water. Notice the method Jesus said to use for believing in Him. "As the Scripture has said," and not because He was putting on a big rock-star healing show, with fog machines and religious words being tossed to the crowd with a mind-numbing beat. I'm not going on a rant of, "Look at all the problems in the church." I'm concerned as to what we are adopting as spiritual based truth. I am pointing out a few things that should be investigated using the word of God. It is true that historically, the church grew and grows in the contemporary season of the times it is in. But hopefully, the growing church is led by the Holy Spirit and not the zeitgeist of the day.

Just because someone comes out with a new personal interpretation of a so-called bible, revelation, or a mystical discovery doesn't make it divinely inspired. Even if the person who wrote the self-proclaimed work says, it came by a vision, dream, or osmosis through a holy man. We, like the Bereans, should seek the scriptures to see if what is written is true. Our pedagogy should reflect the methods Jesus, Paul, and the other Apostles used in teaching the scriptures. They did not teach personal interpretations of the scriptures to accommodate the trends of their day. They continually referred to what the Word of God said, and taught the truth from that pivotal position.

We have been here before on numerous occasions throughout history. Jim Jones, who founded Peoples Temple, claimed he was a reincarnation of Christ and Buddha. The sad thing is that only a portion of the congregation walked out. Shouldn't all the people have walked out because of that nonsensical claim? If your pastor said that he was Christ, would you stay in that congregation? James Warren Jones, and not Jesus, led so many people to their death by drinking the poison Kool Aid. Prov. 14:14a **The backslider in heart will be filled with the fruit of his ways.**

The soulism emanating from the secularism sneaking into our churches has become palpable. We should be concerned if our Sunday services are becoming an electronic event of bits and bytes with pithy and cutesy sayings being proclaimed by a sloganeer rather than a shepherd called of the Lord. I am not saying this is going on in every church. However, we need to check the source of where these trends of pseudo ministries are coming from. We don't need another Sunday with self-proclaimed ministers pumping out uninspired monologues while having a sing-along of hollow praise and worship. Prov. 14:12 **There is a way that seems right to a person, but its end is the way to death.** We need the Word of God being ministered to our hearts and not a watered-down social review of how things ought to be in this day and age.

You might say, "But I feel good when I sing that popular song in church." Good for you, because there is a health benefit to singing happy songs as it releases the feel-good hormones of dopamine and prolactin bringing happiness and comradery. I feel good too, and get some of the same uplifting feelings when I sing along on FM radio, but I am fully aware that it is not praise and worship per se. It is a sing-along, feel-good emotional experience. Don't confuse the feeling of a good body vibe and rhythm with the anointed presence of God. 1John 4:1 **Dear friends, do not believe every spirit, but test the spirits to**

see if they are from God, because many false prophets have gone out into the world.

Yes, it is true that I experience God's intimate closeness as I walk through the day. I see God's hand in so many daily events. But these events do not become the doctrines of belief. These personal signs and wonders that we experienced are the developing love and relationship with our Lord. We may get a personal insight into a doctrine of belief but we cannot build our whole life and salvation on it. It is definitely a great platform to build from, but we are to live the full gospel of Christ by faith. Psalm 12: 6 **The words of the LORD are pure words: as silver tried in a furnace of earth, purified seven times.**

So my friends, what are we to do if we want the anointed glory and not the worldly gory in our lives? Like the Bereans, we should search the scriptures to find our way. The scriptures say to pray for our church leaders and one another. Col. 4:3a **And pray for us, too, that God may open a door for our message.** Eph. 6:18 **And pray in the Spirit on all occasions with all kinds of prayers and requests. With this in mind, be alert and always keep on praying for all the**

Lord's people.

Our church leaders need prayer like never before. They are fighting a battle on two fronts. On one front, the social demands of people wanting their personal sin to be accepted as their human right, and on the other front, the demonic forces coming against the body of Christ. Our ministers need God's leading and help in expressing the heart of God to bring overcoming victory to His ecclesia. Heb. 13:7 **Remember your leaders who have spoken God's word to you. As you carefully observe the outcome of their lives, imitate their faith.**

I have often reminded my students to go and find what I am teaching in the Word of God. I've expressed that they should not take everything I teach at face value, but, like the Bereans, go and see if these things being taught are so. We need the discernment of the Holy Spirit in all that we do, and that includes doing church. Col. 3:23 **Whatever you do, do it from the heart, as something done for the Lord and not for people.** So, I say it again. "Where are the Bereans?" May God give us the heart of the Bereans so that we may be strong in our walk with God, and our understanding of His word. Amen!

AN AUDIENCE OF ONE

Proverbs 5:21 For your ways are in full view of the LORD, and he examines all your paths.

In this world where pseudo fame and celebrity status is pursued at a Herculean pace, many people are preoccupied with building and creating a personal brand for the world to buy into. It has become easy to lose sight of what is truly important. Gal. 1:10 **Am I now trying to win the approval of human beings, or of God? Or am I trying to please people? If I were still trying to please people, I would not be a servant of Christ.**

If we are in Christ, then our lives are lived for the audience of one. Our Heavenly Father is the only one we must satisfy. If we are living in the obedience of God's will through faith, then we are living in reality. Even though it feels good to have the approval of others, we will not need it, because we have God's acceptance and approval working in our soul.

The self-absorption and antics that people

participate in, to give the masses the impression that they've got it all together, have created many ills and dysphorias within people's lives. Sadness, depression, and hyper-anxiety have become the result of this false existence. The healing and recovery that will be needed to restore these people from the effects of these self-inflicted emotional wounds can take a long time. If the Lord is not involved in the restoration of these hurting souls, the healing can take longer.

Most of the time, these people are looking for some sort of affirmation to give relevance to their existence. Therefore, they spend much of their time auditioning for acceptance by everyone - except for the one who matters - God. When people perform for an audience of tens or thousands to be validated as a somebody, they will soon find out that they cannot please everybody. However, when we live our life for the audience of God, then through His Son Jesus, we can please Him by faith and be fulfilled.

In the end, the only thing that will matter is what God thinks. On judgment day, it is only you, and you alone, standing before God. The Lord will not be consulting the so-called status of your social media brand to find out who you are. He knows who we are at all times. Prov. 5:21 **For your ways are in full view of the LORD, and he examines all your paths.**

Thank God, His banner over us is love, and because of that, the Lord has provided a way to receive God's righteousness through Jesus. Sng. 2:4 **He brought me to the banqueting house, and his banner over me was love.** Believing that God wants His best for us, will help persuade us to focus on pleasing God and serving Him with a full heart. The Lord will be our audience and our desire. King David said that doing God's will was a joy. Psalm 40:8 **I take joy in doing your will, my God, for your instructions are written on my heart.** I believe this is the joy of life everyone is looking for, but we will have to accept God's gift of salvation to live in that joy, and have the peace that comes with it.

Perhaps, if we stopped and realized that God is watching our lives and cheering us along, we would be more discerning about our life choices. The Apostle Paul was continually living his life for the audience of one. Phil. 1:21 **For to me to live is Christ, and to die is gain.** "To live is Christ," was Paul's main expression from his heart. The Apostle Paul was focused on fulfilling God's will in his life.

Paul had seen the vain value of his personal religious brand, which he showcased for the approval of the priests of his day. Once he had accepted the Lord Jesus as his saviour, Paul could see the importance of living his life for the audience of one. Phil. 3:8 **More than that, I also consider everything to be a loss in view of the surpassing value of knowing Christ Jesus my Lord. Because of him I have suffered the loss of all things and consider them as dung, so that I may gain Christ.**

Saints, this is the goal of our hearts. We continually press toward the high calling that the Lord has placed on our lives. We live to please our Heavenly Father, who is the only infinite being whose love and judgment matters. Isa. 43:11 **I, yes I, am the LORD, and there is no other Savior.** When we all take our final bow, may our eyes be on Him who first loved us. Amen!

DESIRES

Proverbs 13:19 A desire accomplished is sweet to the soul, but it is an abomination to fools to depart from evil.

Derek Rydall wrote, *"The word "desire" means "of the sire" or "of the father." In other words, that strong impulse to achieve something is actually the "something" already in you, seeking to come out! The very word itself 'desire' has a sacredness about its essence. For the word, De-Sire comes from the Latin meaning "of the Father," to mean that it is of Spirit/God/Source that our desire springs forth from and in that there is a sacred aspect to our desires. Desire is deep love expressed."*

I have to say that when I read this explanation of the word desire, it blessed me. This concept illustrated to me that when God gives us the desires of our heart, the Lord is in the desire itself because it came from Him. Psalm 20:4 **May He grant you according to your heart's desire, and fulfill all your purpose.**

What is your purpose? What is it in God that moves you? What makes you want to shout out to

God and say, "This is what I desire!" What have you desired that has been put on hold because you were not sure if it was of God? Maybe you have wanted to sing, dance, paint or sculpture.

The deep desire to write a book, play, movie script, or even a bible translation continually finds its way to the forefront of your mind and heart but has been hindered by your own thoughts of, "Would God bless me in this desire to create what I see inside of my heart?"

When our heart is for God and the desire of our heart is to bless Him and be the hand extended He created us to be, we can desire what it will take to bring the kingdom of God to this lost world. Psalm 37:4 **Delight thyself also in the LORD; and he shall give thee the desires of thine heart.**

It will take every avenue of wisdom, resources, and creative desire to bring the blessing of the Lord to everyone God has put in our path through a divine appointment. It will cost and it will take faith in the fact that the desires God put in our hearts are part of His plan to bring God's healing word of salvation to all men.

Relationship with God is still the original plan

that God is working from to reconcile His creation to Himself. God did this through the cross and sacrifice of His Son Jesus. However, it will take faith in Christ to bring about God's desire to see all man reconciled to Himself. 2Pet. 3:9 **The Lord is not slack concerning his promise, as some men count slackness; but is longsuffering to us-ward, not willing that any should perish, but that all should come to repentance.** God has desires and He also puts them in our hearts so we walk together bringing about the plans of God. Amos 3:3 **Can two walk together, except they be agreed?**

The desires of our heart are seeds of greatness that God put within each one of us. When we find ourselves wanting something more than the mundane of just existing, then that is the desire of God growing into the plans of God. The Lord brings about the fulfillment of our lives and the reason for our creation through the desires He put within us. We were created in the image of God and part of that image is to be creative. If we are creative people then we will have desires to fulfill the creativity within our hearts.

Desires are good to have. Go ahead and

follow up on some of the ones you have put aside because the enemy of your soul lied to you saying you were being selfish in wanting to excel in the blessing of the Lord.

If you desire healing for someone then call it in through prayer. If you desire prosperity so that you can be a blessing in life, then call it in, and be a vessel of prosperity to the needs you desire to meet. If you desire to build a sky-scraper, stadium, or ocean liner because it is in your heart to do, then do it! The accomplishment of your desires that are fulfilled in God is sweet to the health and strength-building of your soul. Prov. 13:19a **A desire accomplished is sweet to the soul.**

At this point in my life, I desire to write books, publish, paint, and learn the different skills in grafting plants, plus many other life skills. I also desire to help others who have a creative streak running through them bring out that creativity in its fullness to show the world how great our God is. It is time to live and express the desires of your heart and let God know that you are sincere about walking out the purposes He put within you. God's desire is for you to be blessed, now have the courage and desire to embrace God's love for you. Amen!

Norm Sawyer

WHITE-CANING IT

Proverbs 16:3 Commit to the LORD whatever you do, and he will establish your plans.

Although many blind folks see much clearer than people with sight, my pastor used an interesting expression that brought a vivid mental image to mind. He described people who did their own thing that was contrary to God's will - as those who were *white-caning it* through life. Literally, the blind, leading the blind. I could imagine all these people with white canes tapping everything around them and each other trying to figure out what to do next as they followed their personal interpretations of morality and the idea of a successful life. The Lord instructs us to realize that God is in control of our lives, and we are to proceed in His direction with our eyes wide open toward God's plan for our lives. James 4:14 **How do you know what your life will be like tomorrow? Your life is like the morning fog—it's here a little while, then it's gone. 15 What you ought to say is, "If the Lord wants**

us to, we will live and do this or that."

My dream or ideal life goal has always been to own an art gallery. I even picked out the one I wanted in Central America and could visualize what types of art would be displayed in each of the spacious rooms and corridors of this magnificent sixteenth-century Spanish architectural building. There is no reasonable limit to the size of paintings that can be hung and sculptures that could be exhibited because the open grandeur of the edifice could accommodate most artistic creativity and mindsets. I was thinking along the lines that this would be the ideal setting for my creativity to flourish and grow when I start to take it easy in later years. Well, as the saying goes, "Man plans and God laughs," came into play.

It seems that when I would seriously think this idea through, I would get an interruption from God saying, "You have not finished the assignment I have given you. I will let you know when it is time for a new assignment." What I noticed was that when God said, "I will let you know when it is time..." He was not necessarily saying, "It is time to start your gallery." The use of the word *assignment* seems to be loaded with - I wonder what He means by that? Then, I would find myself white-caning it through the thoughts of getting the art gallery together, and the logistics of accomplishing it seemed overwhelming. It just didn't come to fruition. I don't feel hard done by, and I'm not at all dramatically saddened that my vision for my life, has not come to pass yet. No, I am at peace because the direction the Lord has taken me in has been rather amazing. My Heavenly Father has brought me to a place where I would never have thought possible. Prov. 3:5 **Trust in the LORD with all your heart; and lean not unto your own understanding.**

While 1 was looking and considering the possibilities of opening an art gallery, I was led to start writing. Talk about opposite directions. The idea of writing books was not on my horizon as far as I knew. However, having ten books published to date, God's leading brought me to a place that was beyond what I could think or imagine. Eph. 3:20 **Now to him who is able to do above and beyond all that we ask or think according to the power that works in us.** I have not had to white-cane it through the book writing, publishing, or organizing process, because the Lord, in His mercy, has brought the most amazing people alongside me to accomplish what God has set out to do in my life. My heartfelt prayer to God is a request to anoint Miss Jami, Clay, Scott, Masud, and Lee who have put their hearts into making sure my books come out with a standard and beauty of excellence that God can be pleased with.

I'm not saying I would not have been successful at running an art gallery had I gone with my idea of life's fulfilment. What I'm saying is that moving forward in life with God backing me up in book publication has been a healing balm to my soul and has given my heart noticeable purpose in Christ. I might have missed out on the miracle of being able to leave a written legacy for years to come. This has become important to me because there will be a time in our future when what I expound upon and declare in my books as a writer will be illegal and considered narrow-minded in its scope. The Word of God states that in the end days, the governing authorities will not accept the fact that Jesus Christ is Lord. They will justify their maltreatment of me and anyone who ministers the Word of the Lord by stating that we are anti-humanist subversives who are causing emotional conflict by hurting the feelings of sinners because we adhere to the laws of righteousness in Christ.

Biblical eschatology declares that my Christian views will not be looked on favourably by the antichrists of a soon-coming day, and persecution may be part of what I have to suffer through to be a lover of God. As Jesus said in John 15:18 **If the world hates you, remember that it hated me first.** Whether you are a pre or mid-rapturists believer, imagine white-caning it through the end times. What a horror show that will be. I would rather have the Lord directing my steps and bringing me home into His presence, than tapping my way through the maze of a demonic world dictatorship.

Jesus Christ is Lord! and He is the author and finisher of our faith. It would be wise to let the Lord direct our steps and plans for life so that the finished work that our God created us for, is accomplished. Prov. 16:3 **Commit to the LORD whatever you do, and he will establish your plans.** The choice is yours. You can white-cane it through the inventions of your imaginations, or you can walk with your eyes wide open into

the magnificence of God's planning for your life.
The Lord's wisdom be upon us all, amen!

GOD IN A BOX

Proverbs 30:5 Every word of God is pure: he is a shield unto them that put their trust in him.

It must be irksome to God to have people who think they know everything, question God's integrity who does know everything. When we judge God from our human standard, we are demonstrating how dimwitted and ignorant we are because we are missing it; we are deeming God's capabilities inside of our limitations. Mal. 2:17a **You have wearied the LORD with your words. But you say, "How have we wearied him?" By saying, "Everyone who does evil is good in the sight of the LORD, and He delights in them.** They try to promote the idea that God is happy and agreeable with the status quo of our times. When these dispensers of pseudo-knowledge try to expand and explain the idea of God with their inaccurate descriptions of His perfection, they inadvertently put God in a box of distorted ideas of their own making. The great *I Am* becomes a totem symbol of human invention.

History has shown us that we cannot contain the fullness of God within our understanding. The universe cannot contain Him. How then can we think we can constrain God within the limited dimensions of our making? Yet, we keep trying to organize and maintain God within a denominational framework that in most cases has only scratched the surface of just one of God's thoughts. After Solomon had built the temple for God, he rightly said, 1Kings 8:27b **Behold, heaven and the heaven of heavens cannot contain You. How much less this temple which I have built!** What makes man think he can box God up and dispense Him as needed? The finite mind that tries to explain an infinite God will have difficulties thinking things through. We have to respond to what God is doing and not the other way around.

When Naaman the captain of the army of Syria asked to be healed of his leprosy, he had a certain idea as to how the procedure might be done. 2Kings 5:9 **So Naaman came with his horses and with his chariot, and stood at the door of the house of Elisha.** However, when

Elijah sent his servant out with instructions for Naaman to go dip seven times in the Jordan river and he would be healed, Naaman was incensed, and his pride was hurt. 2Kings 5:11 **But Naaman became angry and stalked away. "I thought he would certainly come out to meet me!" he said. "I expected him to wave his hand over the leprosy and call on the name of the LORD his God and heal me!** Naaman had expected the healing to be done his way and within the understanding of his ideology of how miracles worked. People are doing the same thing today. They put God in a box and say to Him, "Work my miracle my way, or do it the way you did for my cousin."

God rarely dispenses blessings or miracles the way we instruct Him to do it. Yes, go ahead and keep praying for the miracle needed, but realize that God works the way God wants so that there is no doubt about where the miracle came from and by whom it was created. Naaman's servants had to reason with him and subdue his anger and pride with rationale logic. 2Kings 5:13 **But his servants came near and said to him, "My father, it is a great word the prophet has**

spoken to you; will you not do it? Has he actually said to you, 'Wash, and be clean'?"

The good news for Naaman is that he did what he was told, and the miracle is greater than even Naaman could have imagined. Naaman wanted to be cleansed and healed of his leprosy, but God had a bigger and better idea in mind. Not only was he healed, but his skin was rejuvenated to that of a young child. 2Kings 5:14 **So he went down and dipped himself in the Jordan seven times, as the man of God had told him, and his flesh was restored and became clean like that of a young boy.** God's way is always better than our ways because God is thinking eternally.

When we seek God's word on a situation and we are blessed to be given an illuminated answer, then to turn around and ask for another word because we do not think the one we got is good enough, or not powerful enough to suit our inflated opinions of ourselves, we need to stop and repent of our idiocy and self-worship. The Lord has all the answers to any question or any situation happening in the universe and He wants us to ask for His help, not tell Him what to do. God wants to be part of our lives because we were created to respond to God's love and friendship. Jer. 31:3 **The LORD appeared to us in the past, saying: "I have loved you with an everlasting love; I have drawn you with unfailing kindness.**

The mystery is, that God will not live in a receptacle of human invention, but, He will live in a human's heart. Wow, what a miraculous concept. The God of the entire universe wants to live in our hearts, and He wants to be invited in the way He has made a way for it to happen. Through Christ, our Lord, God will live in our hearts. How amazing is that? Salvation is God's plan, not ours. Let us submit to what the Lord is doing in our lives and hand over the pathetic images we try to make of God. Blessings to us all.

PART THREE:

QUESTIONS FOR UNDERSTANDING

1. *What did you learn in this section of the book?*
2. *What surprised you the most?*
3. *What subject(s) spoke to your heart?*
4. *Did the material that you read help you understand he subject(s) more or less?*
5. *What topics are important to you? Why?*
6. *How do these articles relate to you?*
7. *After reading this section of the book, what will you change in your life?*

Norm Sawyer

PART FOUR:

SECOND CHANCES

Drowning In Memories

Most people wish they had a second chance at doing things better in life. God gives us all that second chance by accepting Jesus Christ as our Lord and Saviour because all things become new from the moment you say yes to Jesus. 2Cor. 5:17 Therefore, if anyone is in Christ, he is a new creation. The old has passed away; behold, the new has come.

ONLY A SERVANT

Proverbs 14:35 The king's favour is toward a wise servant: but his wrath is against him that causeth shame.

In the poem, *Paradise Lost,* Milton wrote that Satan said, "Better to reign in Hell than serve in Heaven."

All I can say is, "Not so!" There will not be any parties in hell nor good times for the good old boys and their friends. However, there will be a lot of gut-wrenching regrets on an eternal Richter scale of ever growing pain. Mark 9:48 **Where their worm does not die and the fire is not quenched.** 49 **For everyone will be salted with fire.** Separation from all that was ever known and understood will be the reward of a soul left in hell. Eternally left to one's own thoughts of what could have been. The torment of that mental anguish is not understandable to our free and present-day mind.

What Milton said is poetic fiction. The truth is - being a servant in God's kingdom is freedom and life. King David wrote that a servant of menial ranking was in a better position in God's service than anything offered in the establishments of the wicked. Psalm 84:10 **Better is one day in your courts than a thousand elsewhere; I would rather be a doorkeeper in the house of my God than dwell in the tents of the wicked.** Of course, menial in the kingdom of God is greater than anything that could be thought of or gloriously imagined in Satan's realm. The least in the kingdom of God is much greater than the best promotion ever given in the world system.

No wonder Satan rails against God and man. No matter who we are in Christ, God honors us, and we are fulfilled through His love. We are the apple of God's eye. The jealousy Satan experiences because of our anointed position in Christ, causes the devil to break out in a tantrum and scream his nonsense of, "Hell is a great place." What a lose-lose offer Satan has for the gullible. There is nothing the devil can offer mankind that will ever give life or fulfilment. The wages of sin is death regardless if the sin is fun or not. The end game is a hellishness of eternal anguish. Try and reign in an insane asylum and see what you get.

You may be taunted by the devil that you are only a servant in God's kingdom. And on top of that, be accused of the sins of your past and therefore, not deserving of God's love. Psalm 35:21 **They open their mouths wide against me and say, "Aha, aha! We saw it!"** Don't worry, a forgiven servant washed in the blood of Jesus, is greater than the highest ranking and station in hell. As a result of the new covenant that we have through Christ, the lowest servant is blessed in the kingdom of God. Matt. 11:11 **Truly I say to you, among those born of women there has not risen one greater than John the Baptist. Yet the least in the kingdom of the heavens is greater than he!**

"Only a servant," you say! Well, the good news is that we who are in Christ are all servants of the most high God. We do not have to worry about eternal rankings and positions. Luke 22:24 **Then they began to argue among themselves about who would be the greatest among them.** Jesus said those who serve would be blessed. Luke 22:26 **But among you it will be different. Those who are the greatest among you should take the lowest rank, and the leader should be like**

a servant.

I know this is contrary to the world system of promotion and goal reaching. The enemy of our soul would have us scratching and manipulating our way to success. Satan would have us kill each other for the sake of raising our own kingdoms. God has a better plan. It may seem old-fashioned and unaggressive - but trust the Lord's integrity for your life. 1Cor. 1:25 **This foolish plan of God is wiser than the wisest of human plans, and God's weakness is stronger than the greatest of human strength.**

Prov. 14:35a **The king's favour is toward a wise servant.** I would rather be a servant with God's favour in the kingdom of heaven than floundering my way through the maze of the world's uncertainty. God is good, and His thoughts toward us are love, peace, and the joy of our victory through Christ. Let us raise our servant's heart toward Him and thank the Lord for all He has done for us in our past, present, and for what He will do in our blessed future. Amen!

CONSIDER GOD'S WORD

Proverbs 30:5 Every word of God proves true. He is a shield to all who come to Him for protection.

Job 23:12 **I have not departed from the commands from His lips; I have treasured the words from His mouth more than my daily food.** When someone asks me to help them figure out what they should do in a particular situation (and if they are a Christian,) I normally ask them, "What does God's word say about it?" The word says to ask God for instructions, direction, and wisdom for life. James 1:5 **If any of you lacks wisdom, let him ask God, who gives generously to all without reproach, and it will be given him.** The word of the Lord explains how to approach a problem that one may find himself in. You might have to read and do some digging, but you will find the answer because God's word is contemporary, and it will have answers for the confusing and hyperbolic times we live in.

Do not steal was written thousands of years ago, and it still means the same today. Do not bring a false accusation against another person still means the same today as it did when the finger of God wrote it out on stone tablets for the children of Israel. Ex. 24:12 **Then the LORD said to Moses, "Come up to me on the mountain. Stay there, and I will give you the tablets of stone on which I have inscribed the instructions and commands so you can teach the people."** The word of truth does not change, however, we tend to change what we consider truth to be, and therein is the problem and the reason for so many of the counseling sessions that are going on.

If we would just stop and consider God's word on the particular event or circumstance that is perplexing us, we would have fewer problems to deal with. Psalm 119:105 **Your word is a lamp to guide my feet and a light for my path.** We could save a whole lot of hurt in our lives if we would do what God has already said about the situation. For instance, it is not the ten suggestions, it is the ten commandments. That aspect of the word and life has not changed regardless of whether some governmental law has legalized something God says is iniquity. Sin is sin, no matter if the transgression is legal.

Our Heavenly Father allows us the freedom to reason with Him, and hopefully, our choices of reason will result in what God has asked us to do and be, for our sakes, and the glory of God. Hag. 1:5 **Now therefore thus saith the LORD of hosts; Consider your ways.** Interestingly, parents want their children to obey them because they are the parents. However, these same legal guardians reject the parenting of God the Father. Parents have difficulty understanding when their children disregard the rules of the home, but it is permissible for these same parents to disregard the rules of life that God has declared right and true. Can we have both ways? I don't think so. If honouring our earthly parents has a promise of life, then how much more life will there be for us today and evermore when we honour and consider God, our Heavenly Father. Ex. 20:12 **Honour your father and your mother so that you may live long in the land that Yahweh your God is giving you.**

Can God's integrity be trusted? Does God's

honesty hold up, and can it be depended upon? Is God's truthfulness reliable? Prov. 30:5 **Every word of God proves true. He is a shield to all who come to Him for protection.** Considering God's word and drawing faith from it will help in deciding that we can believe God. After contemplating who God is and realizing His omniscience, then yes, God can be trusted and loved with all our hearts. Therefore, obeying the Lord is the right, smart, and divine thing to do. Num. 23:19 **God is not a man, so he does not lie. He is not human, so he does not change his mind. Has he ever spoken and failed to act? Has he ever promised and not carried it through?**

The ability to stop and consider what is said and what is going on around us has become a lost art. Flying off the handle and speaking our mind (regardless of what is in it) has become the new norm. If you want to know anything about the science or facts on any subject, just ask the man on the street. The modern man has become an authority on everything, including what has not been invented yet. Our hubris knows no bounds. Mega information is coming at us with lightning speeds from every imaginable platform there is. Sorting out the fabrications and lies has become difficult to tell from the truth of anything said or written. We need a standard that remains true and forthright.

God's word is still a safe place to get an honest answer if one is looking for truth with a sincere heart. Jer. 29:13 **And ye shall seek me, and find me, when ye shall search for me with all your heart.** There are no gimmicks with the Lord. He is faithful and true to us and will not change His love toward us. Yes, consider His word.

MAY CONTAIN SIN

Proverbs 23:6 Eat thou not the bread of him that hath an evil eye, neither desire thou his dainty meats.

I read labels on all packaged foods. It is one of the ways I have learned to take care of myself and make sure to keep certain chemicals, artificial-sweeteners, and nitrates out of my body. The overwhelming amounts of processed fillers, artificial flavors, and preservatives added to packaged foods as well as to some everyday staples have become dangerous to the point of creating a toxic soup.

I have become so familiar with some of the unpronounceable names printed on packaged and processed foods that I no longer bother eating them. They do not improve over time. They just get more government regulated and more chemicals are added for our apparent safety.

One of the noticeable trends now being printed on labels is the extra warnings of "May contain peanuts or sesame seeds." This added warning has become a common disclaimer because of the severe allergic reactions some people have to these products. The smallest trace amounts can cause some sensitive people to become very sick within moments. We could say as the Apostle Paul says in Gal. 5:9 **A little leaven leavens the whole lump.** Just one peanut can cause major health problems to their whole body.

These people who are allergic must make an extra effort not to come into contact with the said products. They basically have to treat these products like poison or sin so to speak. They must train themselves to be aware of food trends and be vigilant to the point of excess. 1Cor. 9:27 **I discipline my body like an athlete, training it to do what it should. Otherwise, I fear that after preaching to others I myself might be disqualified.**

Many people are becoming food conscious because of the myriad diseases plaguing society. Alzheimer's, obesity, type 2 diabetes, heart disease and disorders of every kind just to name a few. These illnesses are becoming the modern plagues of our time. Unless we take personal responsibility to take care of ourselves, we will be overrun with the deadly effects these diseases are producing in society. If we do nothing to change our lifestyle, then we will end up in a place of paralytic existence, not necessarily living out our old age with health and sound mental ability because of the detrimental effects these modern illnesses have.

Yes, we will all die one day as death is guaranteed to us all. However, we can go out full of life and live out our God-given purpose until the day God calls us home. There is some value in taking care of our bodies throughout life so we can live a whole life within the grace and gifts given to us through Christ Jesus our Lord. 1Tim. 4:8 **For physical training is of some value, but godliness has value for all things, holding promise for both the present life and the life to come.**

Since some of us are becoming avid label readers in order to maintain good health, let us not forget to read the instruction book of life God has given us to maintain a healthy spiritual life as well. The word of God is a living word that can train us to see events in life clearly. As we read His word and make it the authority in our lives, our faith will grow and become vibrant. Rom. 10:17 **So then faith comes by hearing, and hearing by the word of God.** We will be able to read the labels life has on it, so to speak, and recognize the warnings written, "May contain sin."

As deadly diseases plague modern day man, hopefully, we do our best to overcome these ailments for our well being and health. Overcoming sin in our spiritual lives also benefits our health because the result of sin is also death. Rom. 6:23 **For the wages of sin is death, but the free gift of God is eternal life in Christ Jesus our Lord.**

Thank God the gift of life is ours through Christ if we want it. The choice is ours to pursue health in both cases - natural and spiritual. The best part is that spiritual health is a blessed assurance because it is received by faith. It is the gift of God that gives us the wisdom to live out our lives by faith and as healthy as we can by putting our best efforts forward. 3John 1:2 **Beloved, I wish above all things that thou may prosper and be in health, even as thy soul prospers.** May the Lord give us all the ability to read and obey the Godly labels He has printed out in His word for

Drowning In Memories

our lives. Amen.

ETERNITY IS A LONG TIME

Proverbs 29:14 The king who judges the poor with truth, His throne will be established forever.

1John 2:25 **And this is the promise that He Himself made to us: eternal life.**

Through Jesus Christ, we have been given eternal life. We have been made the righteousness of God through the finished work of the cross and the blood of Jesus our risen Lord. 2Cor. 5:21 **God made Him who knew no sin to be sin on our behalf, so that in Him we might become the righteousness of God.** Forever is a long time to lick one's wounds inflicted by a personal choice to disregard God's gift of eternal life.

This incredible gift of eternal value is for anyone who would receive it. What is worth having today that you would give up eternal life for? What is the tradeoff? Wealth, sex, stuff or a new car, house, vacation? What is worth your eternal soul? Matt. 16:26 **What good will it be for someone to gain the whole world, yet forfeit their soul? Or what can anyone give in**

exchange for their soul? Stop, and think, how long eternity is and to be in it without God and all alone. Eternity is a very long time and hard to comprehend within our limited time structure of existing.

God gives us space to repent and take what He says to heart. The Lord gives us time to reason and choose the forgiveness God has for us. Isa. 1:18 **"Come now, and let us reason together," Says the LORD, "Though your sins are as scarlet, They will be as white as snow; Though they are red like crimson, They will be like wool.** It does not matter what anyone has done, no matter how heinous or odious, God will forgive.

God says He gave Jezebel space or room to repent but she would not. Rev. 2:21 **And I gave her space to repent of her fornication; and she repented not.** Jezebel was responsible for child sacrifice, euthanasia, murder and robbery of lands and stock from her own people and yet God was giving her time and space in her life to repent. God is a king who judges the poor and rich alike with His truth and love. Prov. 29:14 **The king who judges the poor with truth, His throne will be established forever.** What more can He do for us? The Lord is open-handed toward us and not tight-fisted. He meets us where we are at and lovingly reaches out and asks us if He can save us. Oh gentle Lord, how marvelous are your ways.

We have all been given plenty of room and time to repent. God has shown Himself to be merciful and kind. However, there does come a time when we have to make up our mind that we will receive what Christ has done for us. Jesus tells a parable of a man who was accumulating wealth continually but had forgotten that time was slipping away.

Luke 12:18 **And he said, This will I do: I will pull down my barns, and build greater; and there will I bestow all my fruits and my goods. 19 And I will say to my soul, Soul, thou hast much goods laid up for many years; take thine ease, eat, drink, and be merry. 20 But God said unto him, Thou fool, this night thy soul shall be required of thee: then whose shall those things be, which thou hast provided? 21 So is he that lays up treasure for himself, and is not rich toward God.** There is nothing wrong with an investment plan for the future, but not at the cost of your soul and relationship with God. Time had run out for this self-made-man because he was not rich toward the God who gives us eternal life.

Eternity is a long time to exist in regret as it literally is forever. God says He put the choice of life and death in front of us. He hopes we choose life because out of His love for us He asks us to choose Him. Deut. 30:19 **Today I have given you the choice between life and death, between blessings and curses. Now I call on heaven and earth to witness the choice you make. Oh, that you would choose life, so that you and your descendants might live!**

Our freedom in God to choose where we will spend eternity is an awesome freedom. Don't waste it on a frivolous, temporary, or corroded piece of stuff that will remain here after you die. Choose life as it is eternal. Blessings to you.

Norm Sawyer

WHEN GOD INTERRUPTS

Proverbs 3:5 Trust in the LORD with all thine heart; and lean not unto thine own understanding.

I was asked recently why a lot of Christians seem to be stuck in the same place they have been for the last few years. No growth, maturity, wisdom, or vision. What is happening and why is this dull passivity being chosen as a way to exist? It seems like a level of maturity is reached and then it dwindles from that point to simply coasting along. Rev. 3:15 **I know your works, that you are neither cold nor hot. I wish that you were cold or hot.**

I think one of the answers is that most people who live a nominal Christian life are fearful that God will ask them to do something they do not want to do. They are afraid God will ask them to sacrifice something they do not want to sacrifice in their lives. Some believe wrongly that if they get too close to God, then God will expect impossible feats of grandeur from them. So they stay just outside of the range of God's voice, so to speak, and allow the volume of the world's activity to drown out God's still small voice. Then when someone gets blessed beyond human measure, they whine and complain these blessings never happen to them.

I am not saying all Christians are living in this insipid miasma, but a lot of them are. What we need to realize is that we want God to come along and interrupt our lives and shake it up so we can be a history changer in the short time we have on this side of eternity. Eph. 5:16 **Redeeming the time, because the days are evil. 17 Wherefore be ye not unwise, but understanding what the will of the Lord is.**

When Gabriel visited Mary with the news that she would give birth to Jesus, her world had been interrupted severely. Luke 1:30 **And the angel said unto her, Fear not, Mary: for thou hast found favour with God.** Change was on the way like she had never experienced. God had interrupted Mary's life and history was made.

Gideon is threshing wheat and hiding it from the Midianites when God interrupts his ho hum day of just getting by on what could be scrounged. Jud. 6:12 **And the angel of the LORD appeared**

unto him, and said unto him, The LORD is with thee, thou mighty man of valour. After Gideon got over the shock of being told he had been chosen to deliver Israel from the oppressors of the day, his interrupted life changed forever. Gideon went from hiding behind a wine press, clipping coupons to meet his needs, to leading an army to victory with the Lord's help.

The Samaritan woman who was dealing with relationship breakdown on a regular basis was on her way to draw water from the well when she was interrupted by Jesus who asked her for a drink of water. An everyday event turned into a life-changing blessing beyond her expectation of life and the men in it. John 4:28 **The woman then left her waterpot, and went her way into the city, and saith to the men,** 29 **come, see a man, which told me all things that ever I did: is not this the Christ?** Come see a real man who interrupted my codependent lifestyle and gave me understanding of my own heart. Come and see this man.

Saints, we want God to come and ask us to do something we do not want to do in our own strength. We want our world changed and interrupted by God so that our lives would be far reaching into the possibilities of eternal grace.

Be encouraged that when God interrupts, it is for an eternal good and not some inconvenience to our shallow lives. You and God are a majority and a great team. Open your heart's ear and hear what the Spirit is saying and let Him interrupt your day. Life may never be the same again. Jer. 33:3 **Call to me and I will answer you and tell you great and unsearchable things you do not know.** Amen Lord, show me your possibilities in me.

NOT GUILTY

Proverbs 30:10 Don't slander a servant to his master, lest he curse you, and you be held guilty.

We feel guilty because we are guilty! Guilty of slander, guilty pleasures, guilty feelings, guilty plea, guilty sin, and guilty of breaking laws. Whether the laws are spiritual, federal, state, provincial, municipal, or social we are guilty of breaking some law - somehow and somewhere.

People feel guilty because they are guilty of sin. Guilt is their default setting in life and a need to be set free of guilt is felt deep within but with no understanding of how to get it done; therefore, they stay guilty as charged. This is why these same people come up with all kinds of self-righteous antics to appease the accusations of guilt that are running wild within their soiled souls. Rom. 7:24 **O wretched man that I am! who shall deliver me from the body of this death?**

How obvious it becomes to those who are in Christ to see the need for a Savior to save and deliver them from their guilt and their personal idea of righteousness. To be pronounced guiltless and sinless by our God because of our faith in the work of the cross and blood of Jesus is an overwhelming blessing within our soul. The peace within our conscience will cause us to bring praises and gratitude to our Lord when we find ourselves resting in the love of God who says we are no longer guilty as charged.

The worldly person cannot see their need for deliverance from their guilt because their scales of tit for tat in life are rigged in their personal favor at best and warped at worst. Prov. 11:1 **A false balance is an abomination to the LORD, but a just weight is his delight.**

The just weight, in this case, can only be justified through Christ and His finished work of redemption. Only God can remove our guilt through His perfect sacrifice. There is nothing within ourselves that can pull it off. Isa. 43:11 **I, yes I, am the LORD, and apart from me there is no savior.**

If we as Christians, are going to be held guilty, then let it be for good works and the destruction of the devil's attacks and agendas. Let us not be guilty of slandering our brothers, sisters, and leaders whom the Lord our Master has redeemed. 1Pet. 3:17 **Remember, it is better to suffer for doing good, if that is what God wants, than to suffer for doing wrong!**

We should be proclaiming what Sargent Shriver said when asked about the Peace Corps' enthusiasm. "The Peace Corps is guilty of enthusiasm and a crusading spirit. But we're not apologetic for it." Yes, I will take that humble attitude into my Christian walk with Christ any day. May we all be accused and found guilty of being a blessing in the kingdom of God. May our attitudes be full of enthusiasm and a crusading spirit for helping redeem all man unto God in love.

Guilt and shame can paralyze our growth in the Lord if we do not put all demonic accusations under the blood of Jesus. Feelings of not being good enough, loved, or accepted are not from God. Eph. 1:4 **Even before he made the world, God loved us and chose us in Christ to be holy and without fault in his eyes.** We have been accepted and made righteous through the finished work of the cross and the blood of Jesus.

We have been washed of our guilty sins

and the charges that came with sin have also been acquitted. We are made new and the pronouncement of guilt over us is now "Not Guilty." 2Cor. 5:17 **Therefore, if anyone is in Christ, he is a new creation. The old has passed away; behold, the new has come.**

The Apostle Peter was riddled with guilt when he denied knowing Jesus. Luke 22:61 **And the Lord turned and looked at Peter. Then Peter remembered the word the Lord had spoken to him: "Before the rooster crows today, you will deny Me three times."** 62 **And he went outside and wept bitterly.** After the Resurrection of Jesus, He encountered Peter and took away his guilt by restoring Peter's heart and setting him back on the Gospel trail so to speak.

Only Jesus can remove the guilt of sin because He paid for it in full. Only the Lord can renounce our eternal punishment because He took that punishment upon Himself. Only God can say we are not guilty because the guilt was nailed to the cross of Jesus and we are redeemed. What can we say but, "Thank you, Lord, for your goodness toward us." Amen.

EXCUSEOLOGY 101

Proverbs 14:8 The wisdom of the prudent is to give thought to their ways, but the folly of fools is deception.

So, what's your excuse? The excuses used to not do a task can take more energy than actually doing the task. I recently got hit with one flu-bug that brought shaking chills throughout my body, a gravelly sound coming from my throat, and dizziness that kept me lying down wrapped in a wool blanket. I slept all day and kept sleeping right into the early morning of the next day. It must have been a twenty-four hour thing because I woke up energy-weak and muscle-sore but I felt a whole lot better. Whatever it was, it was gone.

I normally arrive at the gym early on Saturdays while it is quiet and the place is virtually empty. On that Saturday morning, I was feeling the residual effects of the previous day's bug. I had a good excuse not to go to the gym, but there was this other bug tickling my brain. I said, "Now listen here Norm. If you use the - I don't feel well excuse this morning, then what will be the excuse next Saturday morning, and the Saturday after that?" I'm too tired, I don't have time, I don't feel up to it, and finally, I don't want to go anymore! It does not take much effort to break a good healthy habit.

In our perfidy, we trick ourselves by using ready-made lies to give up on what was once important. It is so easy to deceive ourselves with excuses of all kinds. Prov. 14:8 **The wisdom of the prudent is to give thought to their ways, but the folly of fools is deception.** Before we know it, we are practising excuseology 101 in all our ways. Needless to say, I did go down to the gym and did my best with the energy I had. I was pleased that I had gone and worked out, because I pushed through a lot of pain and stiffness. With God's grace, I felt much better throughout the rest of the day.

We read in the parable of the *Ten Minas,* a master had given his servants money to invest according to the servant's capabilities. The first two servants, without excuse, brought back a capital-gain that was pleasing to the master. The third servant who allowed fear and laziness to direct his actions came up with a grandiose excuse for not working, rather than creating a return on capital. Luke 19:20 **But the third servant brought back only the original amount of money and said, 'Master, I hid your money and kept it safe. 21 I was afraid of you, because you are a hard man.**

Excuses are a dime a dozen, as the saying goes. We can put our energy into getting out of work, or use our energy to complete the work. The energy itself doesn't care which way you go, as the energy will get used up either way. Therefore, use God's energy in your life to bring about life.

In the Gospel of John, we read the story of a man who had been lying in his debilitating sickness for a very long time. John 5:5 **One of the men lying there had been sick for thirty-eight years.** John 5:7 **The sick man answered him, "Sir, I have no one to put me into the pool when the water is stirred up, and while I am going another steps down before me."** For thirty-eight years this man had used the excuse that he had no one to help. Was this possible after all that time, that there was no one to help? Interestingly, Jesus asked him if he wanted to get well. John 5:6 **When Jesus saw him lying there and learned that he had been in this condition for a long time, he asked him, "Do you want to get well?"**

This poor man with no one to help had used that belief as an excuse for his permanent lot in life. When Jesus asked, "Do you want to get well?" He was showing the man that his focus was on his excuse of having no one to lend a hand. Do you want to get well and change the way you have lived and believed for the last thirty-eight years? I'm just speculating, but I think the Lord wanted him to declare his desire to be healed and move forward without excuses.

We all have to answer this same question when it comes to our lives and whether we will continue to exercise our repertoire of excuses day after day. Do you want to get well? Do you want victory over what is holding you back? Do you want to live? Do you want to lose all that weight that is making you ill? Do you want to come out from under your deception and change your thinking? Well, do you? What's your excuse?

Of course, we all want victory in our lives, and we all want to be well and made whole. Therefore, let us change our excuses for declarations of faith, of what we want in the Lord, and focus on that.

Learning to stop the excuses in their tracks before they come out of our mouth would go a long way toward our maturity in Christ. We have to stay ahead of our duplicitous human nature that manifests so easily into laziness. If we are going to cut class, then let it be Excuseology 101, because most people have an A+ in that course. Blessings saints. Be strong in the Lord and the power of His might. Amen!

AN INNOCENT MAN

Proverbs 3:30 Do not accuse anyone for no reason—when they have done you no harm.

There are often lengthy discussions as to how much injustice there was concerning Jesus' crucifixion. Statements like, "He was an innocent man." "He was a good man who did good things for people." "He was a just and holy man who had been framed by the religious ruling class." These statements seem to be the repeated reasons why some folk express that it was unreasonable that the Lord should have suffered so cruel a punishment because Jesus was such a good man. Acts 10:38 **And you know that God anointed Jesus of Nazareth with the Holy Spirit and with power. Then Jesus went around doing good and healing all who were oppressed by the devil, for God was with him.**

Think about it. The Romans had perfected the cruel art of crucifixion. They had been doing it for hundreds of years, and it was a common punishment used on slaves, Christians, disgraced soldiers, and undesirable foreigners. The system was so well worked because crucifixion was a slow death and there was a faint hope possibility of being taken off the cross if the one being nailed had been found innocent before he or she died. Which meant in itself, that there were innocent, good, and just people who had been falsely condemned to the torture of the cross. Not unlike finding out years later that a prisoner on death row had been found innocent after DNA results proved that the person had been wrongfully jailed for something he or she had not done.

What was it that made the crucifixion of Jesus so historically important, world-changing, and eternally binding? If it was only that Jesus was innocent, good, and just that made His sacrifice acceptable to God, then why not accept all the other innocent, just, and good martyrs who sacrificed their lives? There had been plenty of Godly men and prophets who had come before Jesus, who had been killed for doing what God had asked them to do. Jesus talked about them with the rulers of the synagogue. Luke 13:34a **O Jerusalem, Jerusalem, the city that kills the**

prophets and stones God's messengers! Heb.
11:37 **They were stoned, they were sawed in
two, they died by the sword, they wandered
about in sheepskins, in goatskins, destitute,
afflicted, and mistreated.** Why were the lives
of those holy men who were mistreated and
murdered not an acceptable sacrifice to take away
sin?

What we call innocent and what the Lord calls
innocent are two different views of innocence.
As I said, many who had been crucified were
innocent of the crime that got them nailed to the
cross, but they were not innocent of everything
in life or innocent of the sin they had been born
into at birth. Jesus was not only an innocent man
but a sinless man as well. Jesus' sacrifice of His
life was the one whom God could accept because
Jesus was the perfect sacrifice that would cover
and take away the sins of every person who ever
was, is, and will be. 2Cor. 5:21 **He made Him
who knew no sin to be sin on our behalf, so
that we might become the righteousness of
God in Him.**

I agree that it was unjust and insidious for the
religious leaders in Jerusalem to commit deicide

by falsely accusing Jesus and rigging the system to have Him crucified. But God had an eternal plan hidden in Christ that allowed every soul entrance into the presence of God the Father and would allow every person to be accepted and seen as the righteousness of God through Christ if Jesus was accepted as their personal saviour. What an incredible mystery and miracle that had been concealed from the evil one. From the first day after man had sinned, God declared a saviour would be sent to deliver mankind from the bondage of Satan, death, and iniquity, and Satan wouldn't see it coming. 1Cor. 2:7 **But we impart a secret and hidden wisdom of God, which God decreed before the ages for our glorification. 8 None of the rulers of this age understood this; for if they had, they would not have crucified the Lord of glory.**

Had Satan understood the power and mystery veiled in Christ, he would not have instigated the crucifixion of Jesus. When Jesus was nailed to the cross and the moment He shouted, "It is finished," it was finished for Satan and all his minions as their days became numbered. Eternal hell awaits them all. They should have read the proverb. Prov. 3:30 **Do not accuse anyone for no reason—when they have done you no harm.** That same shout on the cross was the beginning of the liberating force that saved us from eternal death. Jesus' resurrection from the dead confirmed life for evermore.

We who are in Christ, have been made the righteousness of God through the sacrifice and blood of Jesus. The Lord's sacrifice allows us to walk as innocent beings before our God. Are we innocent of all things in life? I doubt it, because being human means we will mess up. However, through Christ, we are now accepted as innocent before our Heavenly Father. This is all possible because of Jesus and the finished work He has done for us. What an amazing gift God has given us. Let us be grateful for our salvation that has been paid for at such a great cost. Jesus is Lord!

WHOSOEVER WILL

Proverbs 3:23 Then you will go on your way in safety, and your foot will not stumble.

Revelation 22:17 **And the Spirit and the bride say, "Come!" And let him who hears say, "Come!" And let him who thirsts come. Whoever desires, let him take the water of life freely.** The word *whoever* takes in a whole lot of people and nationalities. The Lord generously sends out an invitation to whoever is inclined to approach God or is even thinking about getting to know God. We are invited to accept His invitation to embrace the love God has for everyone by accepting His Son Jesus, as their Lord. John 3:16 **For God so loved the world that He gave His only begotten Son, that whoever believes in Him should not perish but have everlasting life.** Do you qualify as - whoever? Then you are welcome to believe and accept God's gift of salvation.

Some people think they do not deserve the love God has for them or have the right to ask the Lord for help because they see themselves as - only a .... or just a.... They say things like, "I'm only a waitress. I'm just a labourer. I only collect bottles," and so on. The self-judgment of "I'm just a..." is reinforced by their feelings of unworthiness. The Lord made sure that all people, like the priest, the temple workers, and the whosoevers of the world were included in His covenant. Yes, even the woodcutters who supplied wood for the sacrifices in God's temple were acknowledged by God's law. Neh. 10:34 **We have cast lots among the priests, Levites, and people for the donation of wood by our ancestral families at the appointed times each year. They are to bring the wood to our God's house to burn on the altar of the LORD our God, as it is written in the law.** Lots were cast among the people, as well as the Levites and priests. That's right, the everyday people were included in God's righteous plan for service.

Lev. 6:12 **The fire on the altar must be kept burning; it must not go out. Every morning the priest is to add firewood and arrange the burnt offering on the fire and burn the fat of the fellowship offerings on it.** How could these law-abiding ministers perform their duties without the woodcutters? Everyone is welcome in the work and ministry within God's kingdom, and we are to do what we do as unto the Lord. Col. 3:23 **Work willingly at whatever you do, as though you were working for the Lord rather than for people.** Everyone has a God-given purpose to fulfill, even the crop-pickers, street-sweepers, and sanitary rubbish collectors are all on God's list of whosoevers, and they are eligible through the blood of Jesus Christ to walk in friendship with God.

If salvation had been left up to the human race to become successful, the caste system of life's rankings would most likely be enforced. The majority of the population would not be able to even think of approaching God. We would all have to jump through burdensome hoops created by class structures and invented by fallible men and women who would cause us all to fall flat on our faces. We would end up forever struggling in the trenches of despair. Look at all the cults that are available in this world. They show us the mess that arises when mankind takes over the rules and regulations as to who can have access to salvation. We find out very fast that our flesh dispenses punishment much faster and uglier than God does. As Anaïs Nin says, "We don't see things as they are; we see them as we are." We are flawed, through and through. Therefore, God steps in and offers true salvation through Christ who eternally works for the well-being of all mankind and all the - whosoever wills. Acts 4:12 **Salvation is found in no one else, for there is no other name under heaven given to mankind by which we must be saved.**

It is after a person receives Christ, that their moving forward in life begins to open up to the realm of eternal possibilities. Prov. 3:23 **Then you will go on your way in safety, and your foot will not stumble.** The whosoever becomes a known person in God's kingdom. The whoever now has a name intimately known between God and that soul. Rev. 2:17b **To the one who is victorious, I will give some of the hidden manna. I will also give that person a white stone with a new name written on it, known only to the one who receives it.** Suddenly, just a waitress, or only a store clerk, becomes a king and a priest in the Lord's kingdom fulfilling their purpose in Christ rather than existing in the social standings of the world. Wow, what a transformation from being - just a .... and only a woodcutter, to a soul in relationship with Almighty God. What a miracle salvation is when looked at through the Lord's paradigm.

Whenever man tries to improve the state of the human condition, the task becomes difficult because the foundation that man is building his improvements upon is unstable. When God enters the picture and brings His righteous redemption into our hearts, the amelioration of the human condition excels exponentially because God gives us true life. With the Lord at work within our hearts, we become more than a whosoever. We become sons and daughters of the most high God. We step into our roles of kings and priests ministering unto the Lord. We rise out of the mundane stupor of just being a self-declared nobody to the reality of someone God wants to spend time with.

The Psalmist rightly said in his wonderment of God's interest in each one of us. "What is man that God is mindful of him?" Psalm 8:4 **What is man that you are mindful of him, and the**

son of man that you care for him? For God to take such intense interest in our existence, and to sacrifice His only Son for our eternal lives, there has to be something of extreme value that He sees in the creation of each one of us. The amazing thing is that God's love for us is not based on what we bring to the table because the Lord has already set the table before us. We are to show up at the Lord's table and enter into all that He has for us. The Love of God, and His amazing grace, which is available to whoever wants what God has for them, can receive it by saying, "Yes, God, I want your gift of eternal life through Christ, our Lord." Amen!

JAM

Proverbs 18:9 He who is slothful in his work is a brother to him who is a great destroyer.

A Lee MacLennan saying. "Time gained in laziness is time lost in hard work."

Lee was telling me how he came up with the *Jam Principle*. Lee was spreading jam on bread for his son and some jam plopped on the table. He knew he should clean it up right there and then, but didn't. Later, when he tried to clean it, the jam had congealed and stained the table. The clean up took way longer than it would have had he cleaned up the mess when it first happened.

We have all done this very thing. We have put off something we should have done immediately but left it for later. And true enough, we have all paid for it in spades with different degrees of consequences. Procrastination, laziness, and sloth are enemies of our souls and lives. Prov. 18:9 **He who is slothful in his work is a brother to him who is a great destroyer.**

We do not have to try hard to be lazy - it comes

easily. It's as if being lethargic is our human default setting. To overcome this state of being, we have to stay vigilant to do what God has birthed in our hearts to accomplish. As odd as it sounds, it is easy to put God aside for later - even when the Lord is trying to get us to act now.

How many people are going to get jammed up because they kept putting off the calling of God? I was talking with a minister's son, who was in his late forties. He said he would accept Christ as his Lord on his deathbed just before he passed away. He actually thought he could live a carnal and sinful life until the time of death approached. I said "You can't be that naive to say something so stupid! What if you die in your sleep? What if you are in a car accident that happens in a millisecond? Do you actually think you can outwit God with childish games?" He had no response to my questions because he knew he was putting off what should be done right away. James 4:17 **So whoever knows what is good to do and does not do it is guilty of sin.**

The Apostle Paul was ministering on the Lordship of Jesus and the resurrection power that comes with accepting Christ as a personal

Savior. Like so many people, King Agrippa answered Paul's invitation to salvation with a non-committal attitude. Acts 26:28 **Then Agrippa said to Paul, "You almost persuade me to become a Christian."** Almost - is not a strong commitment to anything.

I almost finished high school. I almost joined a gym to gain better health. I almost tried to get that promotion at work. I almost showed up on time for that appointment. Why doesn't anything good ever happen to me? Perhaps you have jammed up your life with lame excuses, rather than live by a code of integrity. Maybe your attitude has lost its resolve. Perhaps your character has become shallow like King Agrippa's - slothful when it comes to commitment.

What has God been saying to us individually that needs an attitude adjustment to fulfill what He has asked us to do today? When will we act on God's timing rather than - a ho-hum attitude of - I'll get around to it when I feel up to it. My friend, Scott Moore, would say it this way, "If you don't have time to do it right, when will you find the time to do it over?" We only have one life. When will we find time to do it over? Today is the day of salvation, not tomorrow. 2Cor. 6:2 **For God says, "At just the right time, I heard you. On the day of salvation, I helped you." Indeed, the "right time" is now. Today is the day of salvation.**

Remember what Lee said, "Time gained in laziness is time lost in hard work." The Lord Jesus has done the hard work in securing our victory and salvation. Don't let laziness stop you from accepting God's gift of eternal life. The *Jam Principle* tells us - we have no time to be lazy today, because there are no guarantees you will have options tomorrow. Eph. 4:22 **To take off your former way of life, the old self that is corrupted by deceitful desires, 23 to be renewed in the spirit of your mind, 24 and to put on the new self, the one created according to God's likeness in righteousness and purity of the truth.**

Thank you, Lord, for being patient with us. Help us see the blessings you have given us today. Lord, by grace, help us respond to your instructions for our lives. Help us do today what You have sown in our hearts to do this day! In Jesus name!

PART FOUR:

QUESTIONS FOR UNDERSTANDING

1. *What did you learn in this section of the book?*
2. *What surprised you the most?*
3. *What subject(s) spoke to your heart?*
4. *Did the material that you read help you understand the subject(s) more or less?*
5. *What topics are important to you? Why?*
6. *How do these articles relate to you?*
7. *After reading this section of the book, what will you change in your life?*

PART FIVE:

OPTIMISTIC FUTURE

Drowning In Memories

Where there is optimism, there is strength for the future. Through Christ, we can be encouraged to do what God has placed on our hearts to do and be. Phil. 4:13 For I can do everything through Christ, who gives me strength.

TESTED AND APPROVED

Proverbs 22:1 A good name is more desirable than great riches; to be esteemed is better than silver or gold.

I have heard people express what they wanted to be inscribed for an epitaph on their tombstone or voiced at their funeral. I have not thought much of what would be said about me as I would be with the Lord, and nothing said on earth at that time would matter. I haven't given much consideration as to whether it is important what I want to be said about me when I go on to be with my Lord. The importance that some people put upon the impressions they leave concerning their lives made me wonder if I was missing the point of something important in life. Why didn't I give it much thought and why was it not important to me?

What is often said about most men at a funeral is the same old boring thing, "He was a good provider." Of course, that should go without saying, as this is what a husband, father, and provider of home and family is supposed to do - be a provider. In some cases, things that are said are not true. I remember some people expressing platitudes at a memorial about a deceased man I knew well. According to some of the mourners, he was a great father and an understanding husband with a generous heart. The truth was, that he was an obnoxious abusive husband, a brutal father with very little compassion or mercy except for people who he thought he could get something out of. Of course, one does not stand up and shout at a person's memorial, "What a load of rubbish." We just bow our heads and think, "When is this going to be over?" Maybe this is what Jesus meant when He said, "Let the dead bury the dead."

I do acknowledge that this man could have repented for his actions and choices in life before he died, but that is between him and his creator. We never know the heart's negotiations that take place on a deathbed. I firmly believe in the fact that Jesus gives us every opportunity to repent and accept Christ's sacrifice before death. Even if the person is in a coma or delusional, Jesus can get through to them. Titus 2:11 **For the grace of**

God that bringeth salvation hath appeared to all men. Only God truly knows what should be written on our gravestone, because He has been there every minute of our life and has the real account of who and why we are the person we were when we passed on.

As I said, I have not given much thought about what would be the inscription stating who I was, until I was reading Romans chapter sixteen. The scripture verse jumped out at me, and I said out loud, "There Lord, that's it, this is what I want to be said about me when I am gone. I want what is said about Apelles." Rom. 16:10a **Greet Apelles, the one tested and approved in Christ.** Oh my, yes, yes, yes Lord! May it be said that I was tested and approved in Christ. Isn't this what everyone wants? It is as great an accolade as, "Well done, good and faithful servant." Matt. 25:23 **His master said to him, 'Well done, good and faithful servant! You were faithful over a few things; I will put you in charge of many things. Share your master's joy.'**

The reality is, if I or any of us want Apelles' words said about us, then we will have to live up to the statement's value and truth. We will have to come through some tests in life and be approved, reproved, and sanctified throughout our lives to own those simple words. I cannot do it on my own, but Christ who lives in me can make it happen. Gal. 2:20 **I have been crucified with Christ. It is no longer I who live, but Christ who lives in me. And the life I now live in the flesh I live by faith in the Son of God, who loved me and gave himself for me.** What a simple mission statement, *tested and approved* is - when compared to all the epitaphs that are out there.

One day, we will all meet our Lord and maker. I try to have no final judgments on anyone's life because that is the Lord's work. If the things said are honest and true concerning the integrity of those who have gone on, then thank God for the righteous people who have given us an example of forthright living. Prov. 22:1 **A good name is more desirable than great riches; to be esteemed is better than silver or gold.** I am blessed to have found the inspiring words, *tested and approved in Christ.* These words have become a beacon set before me. May we all come through the tests we were created to accomplish during our short time on this earth. May we all help

Norm Sawyer

approve each other in the love of God. Amen!

GRAVITY DETERMINES DESTINY

Proverbs 20:24 Man's steps are ordered by the Lord. How then can a man understand his way?

Someone said, "Rain doesn't fall, it is pulled to the ground by gravity."

Who is pulling you toward your eternal destiny? Are you easily drawn away from the guidance of the Lord by every wind of doctrine because of immature choices in life? Eph. 4:14 **Then we will no longer be little children, tossed like waves and blown about by every wind of doctrine, by people's trickery, or by clever strategies that would lead us astray.** God created us with eternity in our hearts and through Christ set us on a righteous path to follow during our lifetime.

Maybe this is a rigid example, but in the same way a planet remains in its orbital track and movement around the sun, we too have a similar course to follow. The laws of gravity keep the planets from crashing into other planets and keep them from heading toward the sun resulting in a final burn out.

What or who has a gravitational pull on your mind, soul, and body? In your relationship with the Lord, are you allowing God to direct your life's orbit around and through Jesus Christ the Lord? So many people have chosen their own orbital way and have crash-landed with great harm to themselves and others.

In the book of Judges, chapter 14 to 16 is the story of Samson. As I read this story the thoughts of carnal minded behavior seemed rampant as Samson went along with whatever felt good at the time. If God seemed to be the right choice, he went along with God. If girls and crazy living was the event of the day, he went along with that. Samson did not seem to have any sense of direction he could follow except his own brute strength for the momentary problems at hand.

I do realize that in this age of sword wielding justice, talk was most likely the last resort, and true, the spirit of the Lord came upon Samson in order to judge the Philistines because that was Samson's call. However, it seemed everything Samson did always came down to slash and burn then deal with the consequences later. His reckless behavior got him into a place of vulnerability and it cost him his eyesight. Jud. 16:21 **Then the Philistines seized him, gouged out his eyes and took him down to Gaza. Binding him with bronze shackles, they set him to grinding grain in the prison.**

Eventually throughout life, there is always a cost to blatant disregard for the instructions of the Lord. In Samson's case, he revealed the secret of his strength while his guard was down. Samson was no pushover. He was mighty but had assumed he would always be on track with God regardless of what he said or did.

Thank God for the Lord's mercy because Samson repented and was used one more time to bring the judgment of God upon the Philistines. Jud. 16:28 **And Samson called unto the LORD, and said, O Lord GOD, remember me, I pray thee, and strengthen me, I pray thee, only this once, O God, that I may be at once avenged of the Philistines for my two eyes. 30 And Samson said, Let me die with the Philistines. And he bowed himself with all his might; and the house fell upon the lords, and upon all the people that were therein. So the dead which he slew at his death were more than**

they which he slew in his life.

When we stop moving within the gravitational laws, so to speak, that God has put within our lives, we can end up sightless in a worldly prison of our own doing just like Samson. We can end up weak, bitter, and without spiritual sight within the harshness and results of our choices. Many think freedom is doing whatever a person wants without regard for anything or anyone. The laws of life are not like that nor are the instructions of the Lord.

There is a spiritual orbit to life and the gravity of God's ways keep us on track. Is a train free if it runs off the tracks? No, it needs the alignment of the rails to allow it to pull tonnage beyond belief and move smoothly with all that weight. Is a kite free without the strength of the cord connecting it to the hand of the handler? No, the kite needs to be tied to a strong connected cord so that the kite can be maneuvered beautifully in the high pressured winds it finds itself freely flying in.

If the train and kite could talk, they would say plainly, their joy comes because of obeying the boundaries of grace that help them fulfill their purpose. Well, saints, the joy of the Lord and our connection to Him is our strength. The Lord gives us the ability to stay within the gravity of God's pull on our lives. Neh. 8:10b **For the joy of the Lord is your strength.** Therefore, we freely orbit the Son of God and become truly free. Free indeed. John 8:32 **Then you will know the truth, and the truth will set you free.**

Psalm 8:3 **When I consider thy heavens, the work of thy fingers, the moon and the stars, which thou hast ordained; 4 what is man, that thou art mindful of him? And the son of man, that thou visit him?** We are the beloved of God, that is who we are. How can so great a God want our love and friendship? Sometimes I think I know but all I can say is, "Wow, what a good God we serve." In Him, we have our destiny. Keep us Lord in the orbit of your love at all times. Amen!

MAN PLANS - GOD LAUGHS

Proverbs 10:28 The hopes of the godly result in happiness, but the expectations of the wicked come to nothing.

It is interesting when a common saying comes to pass in our lives. "The best laid plans of mice and men often go awry." The definition is simply no matter how carefully a project is planned, something may still go wrong with it.

One of my favorite sayings is "Man plans - God laughs." As I think back to some of the plans I had in life, I must have been a real source of belly laughter for the Lord. The plans I had and the plans God has for me have been cross-checking throughout my life and I have to say, "God's plans are winning out." All I can say to that is "Thank you Lord for your goodness in my life. Please keep leading me toward your eternal plan for my life."

If the world's pulse-rate was being monitored for fear right now, the world would be in danger of a massive coronary. The gnawing uncertainty in life that is filling people's hearts and minds has become unsettling because all the well laid plans are falling apart. Psalm 37:13 **But the Lord laughs at the wicked, for he knows their day is coming.**

There is a sense of a doomsday scenario going on and no one knows what to do about it. As more illustrious and expensive plans come out from all levels of government and worldwide organizations, the more these plans crash and fall into a heap of despair. Hag. 1:6 **Ye have sown much, and bring in little; ye eat, but ye have not enough; ye drink, but ye are not filled with drink; ye clothe you, but there is none warm; and he that earns wages earns wages to put it into a bag with holes.** What is the answer?

When we make plans that do not include the Lord or submit to plans God has asked of us, we end up with insipid and substandard results. Hag. 1:9 **You hoped for rich harvests, but they were poor. And when you brought your harvest home, I blew it away. Why? Because my house lies in ruins, says the LORD of Heaven's Armies, while all of you are busy building your own fine houses.**

When we put God first and choose His righteousness as our template for living and moving forward, He will then put us in a position of blessing and a place of absolute fulfillment. He knows us intimately and knows exactly what we need to be a holy, full, and enriched person. Matt. 6:33 **But seek ye first the kingdom of God, and his righteousness; and all these things shall be added unto you.**

In the book of second Kings chapter six, there is a story of the king of Syria laying plans to destroy Israel. The plans are always frustrated and come to nothing because God keeps revealing the plans to the prophet Elisha who then tells the plans to the king of Israel. Prov. 10:28 **The hopes of the godly result in happiness, but the expectations of the wicked come to nothing.**

In anger, the king of Syria starts to accuse his servants of spying for Israel and asks outright who the spy is. A servant steps forward and points out that it is none of them because God has been telling Elisha what the king of Syria has been planning. 2Kings 6:12 **It's not us, my lord the king," one of the officers replied. "Elisha, the prophet in Israel, tells the king of Israel**

even the words you speak in the privacy of your bedroom. Wow, how true that man plans and God laughs.

We, who are in Christ, do not have to worry about the plans the devil or mankind has against us. We can rest assured in the Lord that He is in charge of our lives and will bring us into a place of absolute redemption in Him.

We can follow the plans God has for us and we can do it with a blessed assurance that God is watching us all along the way in life now, and forever. Jude 1:24 **Now to Him who is able to keep you from stumbling, and to make you stand in the presence of His glory blameless with great joy,** 25 **to the only God our Savior, through Jesus Christ our Lord, be glory, majesty, power, and authority before all time, now and forever. Amen.** Let God plan your next life event and be at peace. Blessings.

A LIVING HOPE

Proverbs 13:12 Hope delayed makes the heart sick, but desire fulfilled is a tree of life.

1Peter 1:3 **Blessed be the God and Father of our Lord Jesus Christ. Because of his great mercy he has given us new birth into a living hope through the resurrection of Jesus Christ from the dead.**

We are so fortunate to have a hope that is alive and living within us. This is not a wishing kind of hoping that maybe we might get something a bit better than we have right now. No, saints! This is a living hope that lets us know we have an eternal inheritance in heaven and a vibrant love that is working out God's salvation through Christ within us. 1Pet. 1:4 **And we have a priceless inheritance—an inheritance that is kept in heaven for you, pure and undefiled, beyond the reach of change and decay.**

We are able to live by faith because our hope is real and established in Christ the Lord. Without a living hope alive within us, faith cannot grow or manifest. 1Thes. 1:3 **We remember before our God and Father your work produced by faith, your labor prompted by love, and your endurance inspired by hope in our Lord Jesus Christ.** Inspired hope produces faith. If there is no hope in God, then our faith will wane and become ineffective.

Without hope alive in our soul that can be seen and lived out, there literally is no hope. When God ministers to our soul, we are filled with hope because His love produces an eternal expectation in our hearts. Lam. 3:24 **The LORD is my portion, saith my soul; therefore will I hope in him.** However, when hope is removed, then so does the ability to love and walk by faith.

We read the effects of lost hope when the reaction of Eli the priest finds out the ark of the Lord was captured by the Philistines. Eli hears that his sons have died in battle. 1Sam. 4:17 **And the messenger answered and said, Israel is fled before the Philistines, and there hath been also a great slaughter among the people, and your two sons also, Hophni and Phinehas, are dead, and the ark of God is taken.**

You would have thought there would have

been a stunning reaction to the news that his sons had died. But the scripture says that when Eli heard the ark had been captured, his reaction was so shockingly upsetting that he falls off his chair and breaks his neck and dies. 1Sam. 4:18a **When he mentioned the ark of God, Eli fell backward off the chair by the city gate, and since he was old and heavy, his neck broke and he died.**

Was it because the hope for Israel had been taken out of the land? The ark held the very presence of God and a living hope to the people. Eli lost hope in that very second of realization when he got the news the ark of God was gone.

This reaction seems to be prevalent because Eli's daughter-in-law went into premature labor and gave birth because of the shock of that same news. She died giving birth, but before she dies she names her son with a hopeless name. 1Sam. 4:21 **And she named the child Ichabod, saying, The glory is departed from Israel: because the ark of God was taken, and because of her father in law and her husband.** She died in pain while losing hope.

The moment the presence of God is gone

from one's life, the hope that was in God also goes away leaving a person without a working hope. How then can faith work in a life with no hope in it? This is why Jesus is the living hope. The hope of eternal life within us is alive; therefore, we have faith in our Savior.

We have hope because we have an inheritance in heaven and in our God. Put your living hope in a living Savior. Jesus is the living hope who gave His life for us so that we would have faith in God and give glory to His name. Psalm 33:20 **We put our hope in the Lord. He is our help and our shield.**

If we have Jesus we have hope eternal, and that hope lives and moves within our soul. Keep your hope alive and give God the praise and faith due to His name. Amen!

I AM A SHORT STORY

Proverbs 15:23 Everyone enjoys a fitting reply; it is wonderful to say the right thing at the right time!

We are called by God to become what and who we already are as God sees us. Finding the path God laid out for us in fulfilling that story is our act of faith toward God's gift of life He gave us. Sometimes my ego leads me to think this world would collapse without my presence making sure all things go as planned. The reality is that I am like everyone else, a short story that is here for a limited time, hoping my life makes a difference within God's eternal plan. The mortality rate for humans is one hundred percent, therefore, we had better get on with what the Lord has placed us on this earth to do. Acts 17:28a **For in Him we live and move and have our being.** We would be wise to start living the life of grace God has given us rather than existing until we finally die.

It is awe-inspiring to hear some people describe with clarity why and for what reason they are here on earth. Their insight into knowing their calling, purpose, or raison d'être with the assurance they express can make one wonder if we might have missed that class on why we are here because they seem to have all the answers for their lives. They want to change the world for the better but many of them end up bumping up against a brass wall when it comes to the strength of character it takes to accomplish such colossal feats they have set out to fulfill. As Leo Tolstoy said, "Everyone wants to change the world but no one wants to change themselves." Therein is the rub. We have to be willing to be changed by God for His use. God's vision of us will transform us into the individuals we truly are and develop our uniqueness that will be expressed through our saviour Jesus Christ.

Some of our short stories are full of formidable challenges and great exploits that overcame arduous tasks. With colourful descriptions of conquering the great beyond, our stories are being engraved into the hearts of men. Other people's stories are sad and describe wasted lives that faded out just as the ink in their pens ran out. We are stories of courageous heroes who gave our lives to God to bless the inhabitants of His creation. While others created horror stories because they insisted on being nihilists who would not accept the Creator's existence. All the while, we are all being loved by God for whose affectionate fellowship we raise our hearts for. Sng. 2:4 **He brought me to the banqueting house, and his banner over me was love.** What an amazing story we are part of.

Every story has a beginning. Gen. 1:1 **In the beginning God created the heaven and the earth.** And every story comes to an end. Rev. 22:5 **There will be no more night. They will not need the light of a lamp or the light of the sun, for the Lord God will give them light. And they will reign for ever and ever.** However, our eternal story will go on with the Lord's infinite plans throughout eternity. What will be written of those times? What incredible mysteries of God's love will there be to discover and experience when no words can describe the wonder that we will live in. Even a thousand poets could not eloquently explain or demonstrate the continual awe we will forever be living in. For we will be alive in the eternal grace of God's goodness.

We may be short stories, but we are part of God's eternal ongoing story that He is writing, and that is the story that counts. Perhaps I can draw an example from the parable of the unwise virgins who did not bring enough oil for their lamps to help them fulfill their relationship with God that awaited them. Matt. 25:3 **The five who were foolish didn't take enough olive oil for their lamps.** Have we got enough anointed ink in our pens to finish our story to the satisfaction of our Lord's vision He has for us and our rewarding fulfillment? Can we finish the story of our spiritual race that is set in this space and time? With God, all things are possible.

Don't let Satan, the evil editor, rewrite your chronicle with his poison pen to suit his corrupted narrative and view of who he falsely accuses you of being. Do not allow the devil, who continuously blames you for sin, to have any space on your holy written pages that are recording your life's journey. No saints! This is our story expressing the victory of our relationship with God Almighty. It is not another hard-luck, woe is me and drawn-out drama depicting people who insist on living in their miry clay. When we hand over our lives to Christ and let Him become our authorized publisher, then our stories will be written in His sacrificial blood which cleanses us from all sin and will debunk any bad reviews the enemy would write about us. Our names are written in God's heart forever. What a story that is and will be. Blessings and peace be on us all.

ASLEEP AT THE WHEEL

Proverbs 20:13 Do not love sleep, or you will become poor; open your eyes, and you will be satisfied with food.

Elizabeth Gilbert said, "Argue for your limitations and you get to keep them."

I'm in my mid-sixties and am aware of what I and my generation let happen on our watch. As we were asleep at the wheel, big pharmaceuticals, agriculture, energy and business stealthily inserted themselves into positions of power, influence and control. These power brokers used lobbyists and methods of campaign contributions to influence legislation in their favor.

We have been lied to, manipulated, and out-maneuvered through planned cunning and we need God's help to see through it all. Psalm 12:1 **Help, LORD, for no faithful one remains; the loyal have disappeared from the human race.** 2 **They lie to one another; they speak with flattering lips and deceptive hearts.**

The only way I can turn things around is to

start with my own life and my own backyard. I can stop arguing for all the limitations I thought were inevitable and out of my influence. I can eat and grow real whole foods without toxic chemicals, fillers, and empty carbs. I can exercise, work out and get busy with living, rather than existing on pharmaceuticals. I can trust in the Lord, rather than the world's best offers. Psalm 20:7 **Some trust in chariots and some in horses, but we trust in the name of the LORD our God.**

Most importantly, I can learn to be grateful and content with what I have, rather than being in debt for the countless range of things being dangled just outside of financial reach every moment of the day. My life can be strong in who Christ made me to be, rather than needing worldly permission to be who I am. Phil. 4:11 **I am not saying this out of need, for I have learned to be content regardless of my circumstances.**

We can all stop sleeping at the wheel and through God's grace and abilities change the world by stepping out in faith, one person at a time. Phil. 4:13 **I can do all things through Christ which strengthens me.** You and God are a majority. God and I are a majority. All it takes is faith in God.

We read the who's who of men and women of faith who changed the course of history and mankind in the written record listed in chapter eleven in the book of Hebrews. These people were men of like passions as we are. They had their fears and limitations, but when they aligned themselves with God's plan and direction they changed the world they lived in.

The proverb says, "Not to love sleep or we will become poor." Yes, if we stay asleep at the wheel we will become poorer concerning our mental and physical health. We will become poor stewards of our lands and properties. If we do not take back our lives from the mundane, we will miss out on the richness of a Christ-filled life. Our strength will be sapped because our heart's focus will wane toward mediocrity, rather than the fullness of a God-filled life.

Wake up! With God, we can change the outcome, no matter how dire things may seem. It is never too late to start changing events in our lives when we work with the Lord. God can do for us in one day what would take us a lifetime to do without Him. 2Pet. 3:8 **Beloved, do not**

let this one thing escape your notice: With the Lord a day is like a thousand years, and a thousand years are like a day.

By God's grace and favor I will not argue for any limitations. Rather, by faith in Christ, I will change my world by believing what God says I can be, do, and have. No more sleeping at the wheel while I go down the road God has laid out for me. In Jesus name!

ALL MY FRIENDS ARE SINNERS

*Proverbs 3:6 In all your ways acknowledge Him,
And He will make your paths straight.*

Luke 5:32 **I have come to call not those
who think they are righteous, but those who
know they are sinners and need to repent.**

I have walked with the Lord for a long time and
am sure, beyond certainty, that I will always need
the Lord to live a life of righteousness. There is
no getting around the need for a savior, no matter
how profound a theology or a new enlightened
idea might sound.

We will always need Christ so that we can
honestly and truly repent. For me and all my
friends, there is no other name under heaven who
can wash away our sins, other than the Lord Jesus.
Acts 4:12 **Salvation is found in no one else, for
there is no other name under heaven given to
mankind by which we must be saved.**

To many, I sound narrow-minded and even
radical when I say what I have said about the
Lord being the only way to our heavenly Father

and true repentance. I am only repeating what Jesus said, and I believe Him since He is the only one to conquer death and tell us about it. John 14:6 **Jesus said to him, "I am the way, and the truth, and the life. No one comes to the Father except through me.**

I have not met anyone else during my lifetime who has even come close to what Jesus has done or accomplished in saving mankind from their sins. We only have to believe in Jesus and what He did through His blood sacrifice on the cross to be restored into friendship with God the Father.

All my friends struggle with all the same problems and temptations that I struggle with. We stand in wonder and dismay at all the tragedies in the world. We know we cannot find salvation within ourselves, and because of that fact, we plunge deeper into need. We can do nothing about it because it is going to take a savior beyond ourselves, who is God, to fix the mayhem man has created through their sin nature. John 15:5 **I am the vine and you are the branches. The one who remains in Me, and I in him, will bear much fruit. For apart from Me you can do nothing.** We need a sacrifice that has been accepted by God Himself. Jesus is that sacrifice.

The world is awash with religious leaders and ideas who claim they can patch up or reduce the effects of sin in life. However, these human beings are limited to their solipsistic views, life expectancy, and geography to have an eternal worldwide answer that all my friends, and I need to be utterly rid of all sins in our lives once and for all.

Jesus, the risen Lord, has dealt with all sins ever committed. Christ did this for all mankind for now and throughout eternity. Grace upon grace has washed us clean, if we accept it by faith. No antics or jumping through hoops of fire to receive this gift of life - just faith in the finished work of what Jesus did on the cross.

As Jesus said, He came for those who knew they needed to repent of their sins. Luke 5:32 **I have come to call not those who think they are righteous, but those who know they are sinners and need to repent.** Those who do not think they need to repent and see themselves as righteous outside of Christ have the same problem a sinner has. They just don't see it yet.

This is why I say, "All my friends are sinners

until they accept the righteousness of Christ." If you are a member of the human race, then you need a savior and Jesus is the Lord of your salvation. Rom. 3:23 **For all have sinned and fall short of the glory of God.** How much is all? All have fallen short, whether you believe it or not.

So, a note to all my friends who were sinners. Jesus Christ made you righteous in Him and because of Him only. Give God the praise and thanks due Him because of all He has done for you. He took our sins and washed us clean, so we can shout with joy. Jesus is LORD! I am the Lord's and He is mine. Sng. 6:3a **I am my beloved's and my beloved is mine.** Amen and amen!

SMILE BY FAITH

Proverbs 3:6 In all thy ways acknowledge Him, and He shall direct thy paths.

Luke 18:8b **But when the Son of Man returns, how many will he find on the earth who have faith?**

Good question. How many will have kept their faith through all the trials and tribulations that are coming against the saints on the earth? I am so grateful that one of the gifts of the Holy Spirit is the gift of faith. 1Cor.12:7 **A manifestation of the Spirit is given to each person for the common good,** 9a **the same Spirit gives great faith to another.** We can call upon the Lord and ask for His faith to be poured within us so that we can confidently walk by faith in what God has called us to do. This is truly a win-win blessing.

This is why we can smile by faith, no matter what valley of darkness we are going through. The facts may be that you are fighting a terrible disease, but God's truth says, you have been given His word that heals. Psalm 107:20 **He sent his**

word, and healed them, and delivered them from their destructions. The facts in your life may find you struggling at every turn, but God's truth is, you are more than an overcomer in all battles. Rom. 8:37 **No, despite all these things, overwhelming victory is ours through Christ, who loved us.**

Asking God for His faith to be at work within us so that we can fight the good fight of faith, is a gift worth asking for. Wouldn't you rather face the enemy of your soul with God's powerful faith? Count me in on that blessing. Prov. 3:6 **In all thy ways acknowledge Him, and He shall direct thy paths.**

Sarah, in her old age, gave birth to a son, by believing God's promise to her. Her faith turned into laughter. Gen. 21:6 **And Sarah said, God hath made me to laugh, so that all that hear will laugh with me.** The years that led up to this miracle were not always easy for Sarah. However, there came the day when Sarah's faith put a smile in her heart, because she had been smiling by faith at the promise God had made to her. Gen. 21:1 **And the LORD visited Sarah as he had said, and the LORD did unto Sarah as he had**

spoken.

We all have dreams and visions that we want to fulfill in this life. By faith, put a smile on your face and in your heart, and keep pressing into God's word for your life. There will be trials and obstacles along the way, but we are fit for the fight. We have the God of the universe living in our hearts. We have the gifts of the Holy Spirit within our grasp if we ask for them. No wonder Satan hates us - we have everything he tried to steal from God. But God, out of His love for us, gave us these wonderful blessings.

When the Lord returns, how many will He find on the earth who have faith? We live in a very secular world-system that makes it clear what side of righteousness we have to choose. It will take honest faith in the Lord to make our walk with God genuine and of Godly substance. We are going to have to smile by faith in a lot of the strange and confusing circumstances that are becoming commonplace in the world.

God was not caught off guard by the events taking place in our time. He knows what we need to get through our personal battles and have victory over the temptations of this present life.

God's gift of faith is needed every day, and I ask for it regularly. By faith, I can put a smile on my face, and walk in the grace of my salvation through Christ who loves me. In Jesus name, may the Lord find faith at work within us when He returns. Amen!

JESUS IN THE FAST LANE

Proverbs 4:25 Let your eyes look directly forward, and your gaze be straight before you.

I was laughing inwardly, as someone was complaining that God was not moving fast enough on their prayer request. This person was wondering why God did not notice they were in a hurry to get this thing done and completed - like, right now! I can just see Jesus pushing his way through the crowds saying, "Hey, get out of the way! I'm in a hurry here. I've got miracles to perform and corpses to raise. Oh yeah, and there is that big bunch of people I've got to feed out in the field." Yeah, right. Jesus in the fast lane. This vision of Jesus doesn't quite make it into my heart. Matt. 11:29 **Take my yoke on you and learn from me, because I am gentle and humble in heart, and you will find rest for your souls.**

We may be all travelling at the speed of light in this world, but God has His timing on everything. Eccl. 3:1 **To every thing there is a season, and a time to every purpose under the heaven.**

Waiting for God to do His work in our hearts can be a long wait if we are fighting Him along the way. Believing God for a miracle takes faith and patience on our part. We do not snap our fingers and God jumps to our instructions.

We who are in Christ must come to God by faith, and not demanding our list of stuff that must be done. We must first believe that God is God and He is sovereign over all of life. Heb. 11:6 **And without faith it is impossible to please God, because anyone who comes to Him must believe that He exists and that He rewards those who earnestly seek Him.**

Indeed, it sometimes feels like God is not moving fast enough on our behalf. Especially when it was God in the first place who put the actual vision we are believing for in our hearts. Sarai could no longer wait for God's timing to have the child that the Lord had promised her. Sarai instructed Abram to sleep with her bondservant so that Sarai could have a surrogate child. Gen. 16:2 **Sarai said to Abram, "Since the LORD has prevented me from bearing children, go to my slave; perhaps through her I can build a family." And Abram agreed to what Sarai**

said. Sarai's fast lane idea didn't work out well at all. God did not go along with Saria's plan but stuck to His own eternal one.

King Saul could not wait for Samuel to show up and minister the sacrifice to God. Saul's troops were starting to desert him, so Saul decided to minister the sacrificial ceremony himself to hurry things along. 1Sam. 13:8 **He waited seven days for the appointed time that Samuel had set, but Samuel didn't come to Gilgal, and the troops were deserting him.** 9 **So Saul said, "Bring me the burnt offering and the fellowship offerings." Then he offered the burnt offering.** Because of this impatient fast lane decision, Saul lost his kingdom, and the events in his life went downhill from this point on.

We are never going to force Jesus into the fast lane of our time table. We have to line our lives up with His plan and timeline. Our focus must be on what the Lord has sown in our hearts and we are to keep our way straight by His grace. Prov. 4:25 **Let your eyes look directly forward, and your gaze be straight before you.**

So many people want everything by yesterday's

date. However, the Kingdom of God works line upon line, and precept upon precept, so that the Lord's plans come to pass in the fullness of God's time. Isa. 28:10 **For it is precept upon precept, precept upon precept, line upon line, line upon line, here a little, there a little.**

Trusting in God takes faith and patience. There have been times in my life when I simply thought of a prayer that I would pray, and the answer to that prayer manifested within the hour. There have been times when the answer to my prayers took months, and other times, many years. What I have come to understand is that when I pray by faith, I also have to trust that God's timing will make all things work for the good of my life and those of whom I am connected with. Rom. 8:28 **And we know that all things work together for good to them that love God, to them who are the called according to His purpose.**

The keywords in the above verse are, "According to His purpose." We can get caught up in the fast lanes of life trying to make God fulfill our purpose. The Lord is the creator, and we are the created. We have to keep that perspective in our life while living out our relationship with

God.

Jesus is Lord, master, saviour and friend. He knows when and what we need. We just have to trust His love, grace, and timing. Prov. 3:5 **Trust in the LORD with all thine heart; and lean not unto thine own understanding. 6 In all thy ways acknowledge him, and he shall direct thy paths.** Blessings to us all.

Norm Sawyer

SELF-WORTH OR SELF-ESTEEM

Proverbs 8:35 For whoever finds me finds life and receives favor from the LORD.

While we are on this side of eternity, we may never fully understand the incredible worth God put on every one of us. Rom. 5:8 **But God showed his great love for us by sending Christ to die for us while we were still sinners.** The moment we grasp some of the never-ending workings of the cross, and what Christ did for us individually, we will explode with unexplainable gratitude toward our God. In that moment of illumination, we will discover our self-worth as seen through the Lord's eyes. The worth Christ put on us by offering Himself as the sacrifice for our sins is immeasurable. God saw us as people worth dying for. Truly an amazing love.

The shelves in bookstores are lined with multiple self-esteem books for self-improvement, self-help, and learning to love one's self. However, self-esteem can only come through a realization of our self-worth. If a person has no self-worth, all the self-esteem books will do little to improve their disgruntled opinions, emotional fallibilities, or muddled feelings of themselves. 2Tim. 3:7 **Ever learning, and never able to come to the knowledge of the truth.**

When we accept the worth Jesus put on our individual lives and come to believe and accept Christ's worthy love for us, then the self-worth we are abiding in will overflow into self-esteem. The fruit of walking in the Lord's worthiness that He has given us through faith will grow into self-esteem and honest humility. Psalm 18:35b **Your right hand supported me, and your gentleness made me great.** How can we not give glory to our heavenly Father, for the loving gift of self-worth He has given us?

Living from a position of feeling worthless, many people in the world are trying to prove to God how much they love Him. Some do it through declarations of humanistic laws that are humanly impossible to keep, and some bring their religious fervor into extreme outrageousness by blowing people up in the name of God. Prov. 10:20b **The mind of the wicked is of little worth.** All in the hope of being accepted by God. Meanwhile,

God has already given the world His Son, Jesus, as the acceptable sacrifice for all of mankind to find their lives and live in God's holy worthiness.

The Apostle John had an understanding of his self-worth. In the Gospel of John, in five different verses, John refers to himself as, "The disciple, whom Jesus loved." Rather than John putting his full trust in the love he had for Jesus, John put his full trust in the love that Jesus had for John. The self-worth that John had gleaned because of the love he knew Jesus had for him, gave John the ability to become the Apostle of love. God wants us to trust in His love for us. That is where the self-worth of our life will become a strong foundation for living in Christ. Knowing who we are in Christ makes all the difference in our daily walk with God.

We can read hundreds of self-esteem books and never find the self-worth we are looking for. When we acknowledge how worthy the name of Jesus is, then we will find our selves in His perfect name. What an amazing Lord we have. Christ gave us our worth through His divine deity. Only God, who loves us, could have made this miracle come true for our lives. Thank you, Lord, for giving my soul eternal value in Christ. What an amazing grace we have been given.

Norm Sawyer

PART FIVE:

QUESTIONS FOR UNDERSTANDING

1. *What did you learn in this section of the book?*
2. *What surprised you the most?*
3. *What subject(s) spoke to your heart?*
4. *Did the material that you read help you understand the subject(s) more or less?*
5. *What topics are important to you? Why?*
6. *How do these articles relate to you?*
7. *After reading this section of the book, what will you change in your life?*

ABOUT THE AUTHOR

I have been in Christian ministry in one form or another for about forty years. I attended Commonwealth Bible College in Katoomba, New South Wales, Australia, in 1980. Ministry at that time involved prison ministries, preaching on the radio in a small town, and church-related works of all kinds. I have taught bible college courses and also have been involved in personal discipleship training. God has blessed me all along the way. Now I have the opportunity to write down what was experienced throughout the years. The Lord has blessed me with sound and forthright material to write a series of Christian devotionals. I have lived the testimonies on these pages and can attest to the fact that God is so faithful and good. My hope is that your soul will be enriched as you read this book. God bless you.

CONNECT WITH NORM

Norm's Blog "Sir Norm's Proverbial Comment" can be found online in English, French and Spanish. Your comments on any of the hundreds of blog posts are appreciated.

www.sirnorm.com